TIME ZONES

Catherine Frazier
Richard Frazier
Jennifer Wilkin

SECOND EDITION

NATIONAL GEOGRAPHIC LEARNING | CENGAGE Learning

Australia • Brazil • Japan • Korea • Mexico • Singapore • Spain • United Kingdom • United States

Time Zones Student Book 2
Second Edition

Catherine Frazier, Richard Frazier, and Jennifer Wilkin

Publisher: Andrew Robinson

Executive Editor: Sean Bermingham

Senior Development Editor: Derek Mackrell

Development Editors: Sian Mavor,
   Charlotte Sharman

Assistant Editor: Melissa Pang

Director of Global Marketing: Ian Martin

Product Marketing Manager: Anders Bylund

Media Researcher: Leila Hishmeh

Senior Director of Production:
   Michael Burggren

Senior Content Project Manager:
   Tan Jin Hock

Manufacturing Planner:
   Mary Beth Hennebury

Compositor: Cenveo Publisher Services

Cover/Text Design: Creative Director:
   Christopher Roy, Art Director: Scott Baker,
   Senior Designer: Michael Rosenquest

Cover Photo: John Coletti/JAI/Corbis

Student Book with Online Workbook:
ISBN-13: 978-1-305-51072-2

Student Book:
ISBN-13: 978-1-305-25985-0

National Geographic Learning
20 Channel Center Street
Boston, MA 02210
USA

Cengage Learning is a leading provider of customized learning solutions with employees residing in nearly 40 different countries and sales in more than 125 countries around the world. Find your local representative at:
www.cengage.com

Cengage Learning products are represented in Canada by Nelson Education, Ltd.

Visit National Geographic Learning online at **NGL.Cengage.com**

Visit our corporate website at **www.cengage.com**

Printed in China
4 5 6 7 8 9 20 19 18 17

Contents

SCOPE AND SEQUENCE

1

WHAT DO YOU LIKE TO DO?

Preview

A **Look at the photo.** Complete the caption.

> practicing   do sports   hobby

B **🎧1-01 Listen.** Complete the sentences.

play tennis   do origami   collect comic books   play the guitar   draw

1. Tracey likes to _____ . It's a kind of paper art.

2. Daniel likes to _____ . He buys them online.

3. Sara likes to _____ . She does it twice a week.

4. Chris likes to _____ and _____ , but he doesn't like sports.

C **Talk with a partner.** What hobbies do you have?

> What do you like to do?

> I like to draw.

> Cool. What other things do you like to do?

> I like to play the guitar.

These boys like to _____ on the weekend. Their _____ is motocross. They are _____ for a race.

Language Focus

A 🎧1-02 **Listen and read.** Then repeat the conversation and replace the words in blue.

REAL ENGLISH I'm good.

B **Practice with a partner.** Replace any words to make your own conversation.

🎧1-03

TALKING ABOUT HOBBIES

What do you like to do on weekdays / on weekends?	I like to play sports.
Do you like to collect things?	Yes, I do. No, I don't.
How often do you play soccer?	I play once / twice / three times a week. I never play soccer.
When do you do karate?	I do it before / after school.

C 🎧 1–04 **Listen.** Complete the conversation.

Ming: Nadine, what do you do (1) _____ school?

Nadine: Well, I play volleyball and I go to (2) _____ class.

Ming: Really? How often do you play volleyball?

Nadine: I play (3) _____ times a week, Mondays to Wednesdays. My guitar classes are on the other days.

Ming: What do you do before school on weekdays?

Nadine: I play soccer once a week, on (4) _____.

Ming: What do you like to do on weekends?

Nadine: I do karate on (5) _____. On Sundays, I do homework!

IDIOM

"Once bitten, twice shy" means to be ____ about something after a bad experience.

a. angry
b. sad
c. careful

D **Complete Nadine's schedule.** Use the information in **C**.

TIME	MONDAY	TUESDAY	WEDNESDAY	THURSDAY	FRIDAY	SATURDAY	SUNDAY
7:00–8:00							
8:00–3:00			school				
3:00–5:00	volleyball			guitar class	guitar class		

E **Work with a partner.** Complete the *Questions* column of the chart on your own. Then take turns to ask your partner questions. Write his or her answers in the *Answers* column.

QUESTIONS	ANSWERS
1. What do you like to do after school?	
2. Do you like to . . .	
3. How often do you . . .	
4.	
5.	

The Real World

Robot
Scientist

Chad Jenkins is a National Geographic Explorer. He studies how robots can learn and work with humans.

A **Complete the sentences.** Use the words in the box.

> learn   dangerous   different   carry   messy   tasks

Some (1) _____ are difficult or (2) _____ for people. But robots can help us with them. There are many (3) _____ kinds of robots. Some help us to clean a (4) _____ house or (5) _____ heavy things. Some robots help us (6) _____ more about places outside Earth.

B 🎧1-05 **Listen.** Check (✓) the things that Jenkins' robot can do.

☐ play video games   ☐ read comics   ☐ dance

☐ set the table   ☐ clean the room   ☐ play music

CRITICAL THINKING   What would you like robots to do for you?

Pronunciation

Reduction: *to*

A 🎧 1–06 **Listen and repeat.**

1. What do you like to do?
2. Does she like to draw?
3. I like to play tennis.
4. I don't like to play sports.

B 🎧 1–07 **Listen.** Complete the sentences.

1. What do you _____ ?
2. Do you _____ the piano?
3. I _____ karate.
4. My parents _____ Korean food.
5. My mother doesn't _____ every day.

C **Work with a partner.** Take turns to read the sentences in **B.**

DO YOU KNOW?

Karate is a martial art from ____ .

a. China
b. Japan
c. Korea

Communication

Share your schedule. Work with a partner. **Student A:** Complete the schedule below. Don't show your partner. Ask and answer questions about your partner's schedule.
Student B: Turn to page 130 and follow the instructions.

TIME	MONDAY	TUESDAY	WEDNESDAY	THURSDAY	FRIDAY
Before school					
Morning			English	math	
			lunch		
Afternoon	English				homework
After school		soccer			

When do you have math class?

I have math class on Tuesday mornings.

How often do you play soccer?

I never play soccer.

Cécilia Cassini wearing
the clothes she made

Reading

A The article is about three children's _____ .

a. hobbies   b. clothes   c. books

B **Scan the article.** Match the people to their hobbies.

1. Cécilia   ○   ○ a. takes photos

2. Hawkeye ○   ○ b. plays drums

3. Malachi   ○   ○ c. makes clothes

C **Scan the article again.** When did they start their hobbies? Underline their ages.

INCREDIBLE KIDS

🎧 1–08

These children are doing amazing things.

Cécilia Cassini likes to wear beautiful clothes. She also likes to make clothes. She does her homework in school at recess every day. After school, she likes to sew! Cécilia started to sew at age six. Her designs
5 are famous. Sometimes she makes dresses for famous people like Taylor Swift. She also makes clothes for poor children.

Hawkeye Huey likes to take photos. He started his hobby when he was only four. Hawkeye uses an instant camera to take photos. He takes many photos of people and places. Hawkeye's father, Aaron,
10 created an Instagram account for him and posts his photos there. The account has more than 60,000 followers! Aaron also takes Hawkeye to different places to take photos. He says it's great for Hawkeye to meet different people and see their way of life.

Malachi Samedy likes to collect comic books and play computer
15 games. But Malachi loves to play the drums more than anything else. At age two, he got his first drum set. At age four, he went to music school. Now he performs all over the world by himself and with famous musicians. He likes to perform for other children. He also wants to teach children from around the world to play the drums.
20 He wants to inspire them to try new things.

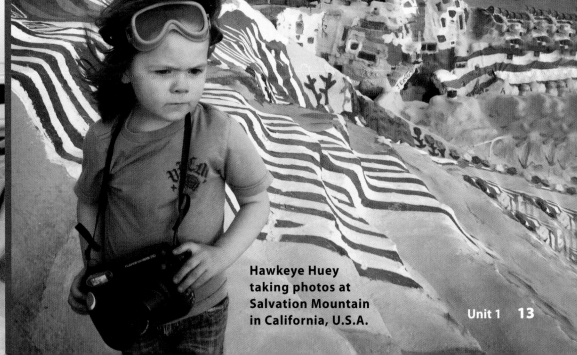

Hawkeye Huey taking photos at Salvation Mountain in California, U.S.A.

Comprehension

A **Answer the questions about** *Incredible Kids.*

1. Detail Cécilia makes clothes for _____ .

   a. her pets   b. adults and children   c. children only

2. Reference In line 10, "him" refers to _____ .

   a. Hawkeye   b. Aaron   c. a person Hawkeye met

3. Inference Aaron thinks photography can help Hawkeye learn about _____ .

   a. people's hobbies   b. traveling   c. people different from him

4. Detail Malachi's favorite hobby is _____ .

   a. collecting comic books   b. playing the drums   c. helping other children

5. Vocabulary To "inspire" means to _____ to do something. (line 20)

   a. order someone   b. ask for help   c. make someone want

B **Work with a partner.** Check (✓) the correct person. More than one answer is possible.

Who . . .	Cécilia	Hawkeye	Malachi
1. helps other children?			
2. started their hobby before they were five?			
3. works with famous people?			
4. takes photographs of people and places?			

C **Talk with a partner.** Which person do you think is the most amazing? Why?

Writing

Write an email. Tell a friend about your hobbies and interests.

From: **Amy**   To: **Sophia**

Subject: How are you?

Hi Sophia!

It's Amy from Australia. I have a new hobby. It's playing the guitar. I like to play the guitar a lot. I play after school with my friends. What are your hobbies? Do you like music? Write back soon!

Amy

Bird Girl

ABOUT THE VIDEO

Mary Lou makes some new friends after moving to her new home.

BEFORE YOU WATCH

Talk with a partner. How many different kinds of birds do you know?

WHILE YOU WATCH

A **Check (✓) the things that Mary Lou likes to do.**

Mary Lou likes to _____.

- ◯ watch birds
- ◯ keep pet birds
- ◯ write about birds
- ◯ draw birds
- ◯ make songs about birds

B **Watch the video again.** Circle **T** for True or **F** for False.

1. Mary Lou became interested in birds at school.   **T F**
2. Mary Lou usually watches birds at the zoo.   **T F**
3. Mary Lou learns about birds on the Internet.   **T F**
4. Mary Lou still likes to do the same things as other children.   **T F**

AFTER YOU WATCH

Talk with a partner. What kind of birds can you see in your country? Do you think bird watching is an interesting hobby?

A bird watcher

WHAT DOES SHE LOOK LIKE?

Preview

A 🎧1-09 **Listen.** Circle the words you hear.

1. Person A has (**long** / **short**) red hair. _____

2. Person B has (**wavy** / **curly**) brown hair. _____

3. Person C has (**blond** / **black**) hair and (**green** / **blue**) eyes. _____

4. Person D has (**black** / **brown**) hair and (**blue** / **brown**) eyes. _____

5. Person E has (**spiky** / **short**) black hair and (**brown** / **green**) eyes. _____

B **Look at the photos.** Find people to match the descriptions in **A.** Write the numbers.

C **Work with a partner.** Choose three people in the photos and write notes about them. Describe the people to your partner.

PERSON			
DESCRIPTION			

This person is male. He has short black hair.

Is it Person 2?

1. straight blond hair
2.
3. long black hair
4. short black hair brown eyes
5.
6.
7. short brown hair blue eyes
8.
9.
10.
11.
12.
13.
14.
15. short, curly red hair
16.
17.
18. curly brown hair
19.
20.

Language Focus

A 🎧1–10 **Listen and read.** Then repeat the conversation and replace the words in blue.

REAL ENGLISH · I'm on my way.

B **Practice with a partner.** Replace any words to make your own conversation.

1. Ming, I'm at the **soccer** game now. Where are you?
   Sorry, I'm late. I'm on my way. Do you see Emily?
   hockey / rugby

2. She has **short blond** hair and **blue** eyes.
   Emily? What does she look like?
   straight black / brown · spiky red / green

3. Does she wear glasses?
   No, she doesn't. I think she's wearing **a red T-shirt**.
   Oh, I see her!
   blue pants / a green shirt

4. **Excuse me**, are you Emily? I'm . . . Oh! It's you, Stig!
   Hello / Hi there

🎧 1–11

DESCRIBING PEOPLE

What **does** he **look like**?	He's **tall** and he has **short**, **curly hair**.
What **do** you **look like**?	I'm **short** and I have **long**, **straight red hair**. I **have braces** and I **wear glasses**. I'm **medium height** and I **have freckles**.

C **Look at the photo above.** Complete the sentences.

> short   curly   wavy   medium height
> brown   blond   glasses

1. He's tall and has _____ brown hair.

2. She's _____ and she has straight hair.

3. She's _____ and she has curly _____ hair.

   She wears _____, too.

4. He has _____ brown hair.

5. She's tall and has _____ hair.

IDIOM

"I couldn't keep a straight face" means
I _____.
a. cried
b. laughed
c. talked

D 🎧 1–12 **Listen.** Complete the conversations.

1. Joyce: Hey, there's a new boy in class.

   Ben: Oh, really? What does he (1) _____?

   Joyce: He's (2) _____ and he has (3) _____ hair.

2. Mike: Do you see my sisters?

   Tina: (4) _____ look like?

   Mike: They wear (5) _____ and they have (6) _____.

E **Work with a partner. Student A:** Choose a famous person. Describe him or her to your partner. **Student B:** Guess the famous person.

> This person is an actress and a singer. She's medium height. She has long, curly brown hair. She has big brown eyes.

> Is it Selena Gomez?

Mind Power

Tan Le is a National Geographic Explorer. She wants to help people learn more about how their brains work. Her device, the Emotiv Insight, helps people to have better, healthier lives.

A man using the Emotiv Insight

A **Work with a partner.** Read the information above. Look at the photos. What do you think Tan Le's device does?

B 🎧 1–13 **Listen.** Circle **T** for True or **F** for False.

1. The Emotiv Insight collects information on your heart.   **T**   **F**

2. The Emotiv Insight lets you drive without using your hands.   **T**   **F**

3. The Emotiv Insight changes your physical appearance.   **T**   **F**

4. The Emotiv Insight is useful for studying our brains.   **T**   **F**

CRITICAL THINKING Do you think this invention is useful? How can it help people have healthier lives?

Pronunciation

Consonant blends: *bl, br, gl, gr*

A 🎧 1–14 **Listen and repeat.**

1. blue 2. brown 3. glasses 4. gray

B 🎧 1–15 **Listen.** Circle the sounds you hear.

1. gr br 2. gl bl 3. gl bl 4. br gr
5. bl gl 6. gr br 7. gr br 8. gr br

C **Work with a partner.** Take turns to read the words below.

1. braces 2. grow 3. glad 4. blink
5. bring 6. blow 7. global 8. greet

Communication

Play a guessing game. Look at the photo on page 130. **Student A:** Choose one person in the photo. Don't tell your partner who it is. **Student B:** Ask yes/no questions to guess who your partner chose. Take turns.

Does the person have black hair?

Does the person wear glasses?

Yes!

No.

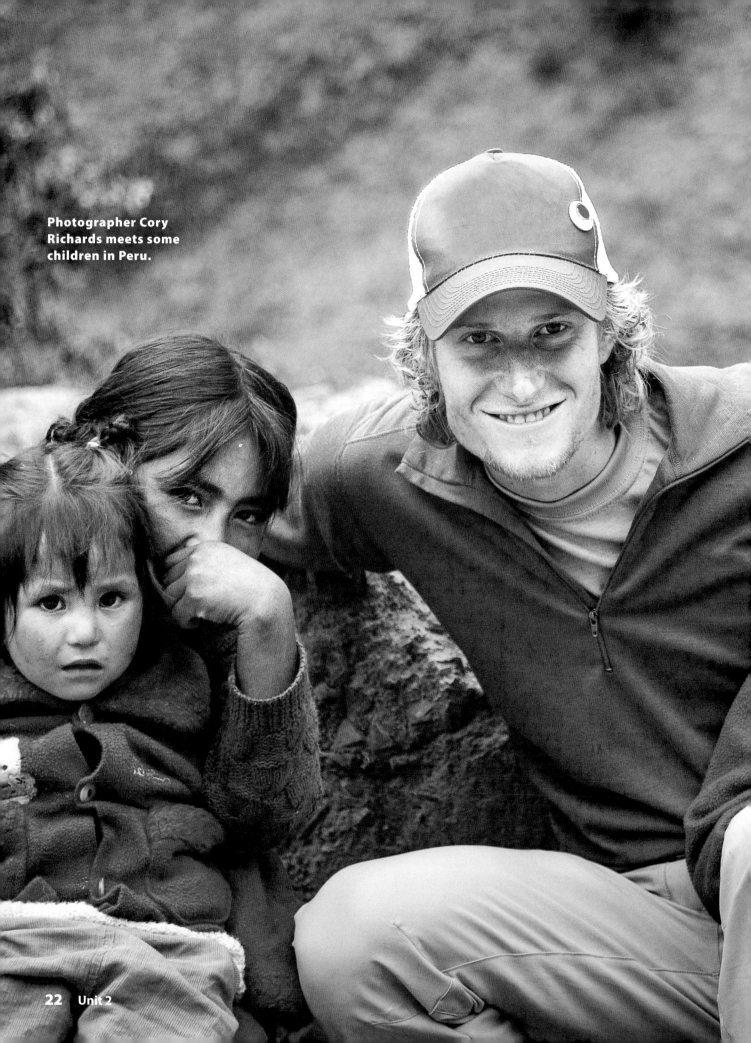

Photographer Cory Richards meets some children in Peru.

Reading

A **Look at the photo.** What do you think these people are like?

B **Skim the article.** When do people create a first impression?

    a. when they meet someone new

    b. when they know someone well

C **Scan the article.** When is a good first impression important?

FIRST IMPRESSIONS

🎧 1–16

We look at people's physical appearance, such as eyes, hair, and height, all the time. When we meet someone we don't know, we create an idea of what that person is like in our mind. This is called a first impression.

5 How do we create first impressions of people? Most of the time, we see what the person looks like. For example, we may think that a person wearing glasses looks smart.

A writer, Malcolm Gladwell, wrote about how we make decisions using our first impressions. He did a survey of the leaders of big 10 companies in the United States. He found that a lot of them were tall men—about 1.8 meters. Most men in the United States are about 1.75 meters tall. Gladwell says that we choose taller people to be our leaders without knowing it. This is because tall people feel like leaders to us. But not everyone agrees. We don't always make 15 important decisions based on only our first impressions.

Giving people a good first impression can be important, like in a job interview. But first impressions are not always true. We often change how we feel about people when we know them better.

Comprehension

A **Answer the questions about *First Impressions*.**

1. `Vocabulary` An impression is a(n) _____ .

   a. person   b. idea   c. object

2. `Detail` We usually create first impressions based on people's _____ .

   a. jobs   b. names   c. physical appearance

3. `Reference` In line 10, "them" refers to the _____ .

   a. leaders   b. big companies   c. people in the United States

4. `Inference` Tall people feel like leaders because they look _____ .

   a. smart   b. powerful   c. friendly

5. `Detail` According to the article, first impressions are sometimes _____ .

   a. difficult   b. interesting   c. incorrect

B **Match.** Join the main ideas to their explanations.

1. We usually create first impressions of others by seeing what they look like.   ○

2. We can't always tell what someone is like by his or her physical appearance.   ○

3. Giving people a good first impression is important.   ○

○ a. People can look or feel different by changing their hairstyles or their clothes.

○ b. When we talk to people we meet for the first time, we usually want them to think of us in a good way.

○ c. We look at their faces, their hair, or the clothes they wear.

C **Talk with a partner.** Talk about a time when your first impression of someone was wrong.

Writing

Write a short paragraph. Describe yourself or someone you know.

I'm tall and I wear glasses. I have short, curly blond hair, just like my mom. But I have green eyes like my dad. I don't have freckles. I wear braces.

VIDEO

Great Facial Hair

BEFORE YOU WATCH

Look at the pictures below. Write the names of the mustache and beard styles.

> pencil   musketeer   dali   toothbrush   full beard

1. _____

2. _____

3. _____

4. _____

5. _____

A participant of the World Beard and Mustache Championships shows off his beard.

WHILE YOU WATCH

A Circle the mustaches and beards above that you see.

B Watch the video again. Circle the correct answers.

1. The competition takes place every (**year** / **two years**).

2. John has a (**brown** / **white**) beard.

3. Leo has a long, (**curly** / **straight**) black mustache.

4. Jack Passion won the competition with his (**short brown** / **long red**) beard.

AFTER YOU WATCH

Talk with a partner. Does anyone in your family have a beard or mustache? What's it like? Why do you think some people want to grow a beard or a mustache?

I BOUGHT NEW
SHOES!

Preview

A 🎧 1-17 **Listen.** Number the clothing items.

watch _____   dress _____   glasses _____   T-shirt _____

skirt _____   pants _____   jacket _____   shoes _____

B Group the clothing items in A.

Tops _____

Footwear _____

Bottoms _____

Accessories   watch _____

C Talk with a partner. Look at the photo. What are the people wearing? What do you like to wear?

What do you like to wear on weekends?

I like to wear T-shirts, jeans, and a hat.

A group of teens on
the train in Taipei

Language Focus

A 🎧 1–18 **Listen and read.** Then repeat the conversation and replace the words in blue.

REAL ENGLISH What's wrong?

B **Practice with a partner.** Replace any words to make your own conversation.

1 Are you ready, Maya?

No! I don't have anything to wear to the **party**.

barbecue
dance

2 But you went shopping **last week**.

Yeah, and I bought a nice blue skirt.

two days ago
on Saturday

3 OK, great. Do you have **a top**?

Yes, my mom gave me **a new top** a few days ago.

a blouse / a new blouse
any shoes / some new shoes

4 So, **what's wrong**?

My outfit looks like a school uniform!

what's the problem
what's the matter

🎧 1–19

TALKING ABOUT SHOPPING

I like your sweater. Did you get it recently?	Yes, I bought it	last	weekend. night. week. month.
Are those new sneakers?	Yes, I just bought them	two days a week	ago.
	No, I bought them	a couple of months a year	

C **Complete the sentences.** Use *last* or *ago*. Then answer the questions.

Ben, Maria, and Sue went to a party (1) _____ night. Ben wore a cool T-shirt, black

pants, and a new jacket. He bought his jacket a week (2) _____ at the mall. He got

his T-shirt (3) _____ summer and the pants a year (4) _____ . Maria wore a

white top and a new red skirt. She got the top (5) _____ month. Her skirt was

expensive. Her aunt bought it for her three weeks (6) _____ . Sue wore a beautiful

new dress. She bought it online two days (7) _____ , just in time for the party.

1. When did Ben buy his jacket? He bought it _____ .

2. Did Maria get her skirt last week? _____ .

3. Did Sue get her dress recently? _____ .

D 🎧 1–20 **Complete the conversation.** Write the correct forms of the verbs and a time
expression with *last* or *ago*. Then listen and check your answers.

Paula: Dad, I need new clothes for school.

Dad: But you already have so many clothes. What about that blue dress you have?

Paula: Dad, I (1) _____ (**buy**) that dress (2) _____ (**two years**).
       It's too small now.

Dad: Okay, how about this green blouse?

Paula: Mom (3) _____ (**give**) it to me (4) _____ (**summer**),
       but I tore it (5) _____ (**a week**)!

Dad: All right. Let's go shopping this weekend.

E **Play a chain game.** Work in a group. Name the last item
of clothing you bought and when you bought it.
Your group members continue the chain.

> I bought a red shirt last weekend.

> Jun bought a red shirt last weekend.
> I got new sneakers a month ago.

School Uniforms

Do you wear a school uniform?
Many students around the world
wear a school uniform. It can help
to make everyone feel part of a
team. Christ's Hospital, a school in
England, has a special uniform.

A Match the parts of the school uniform in
the photo.

coat _____   skirt   _____
socks _____   neckband _____

B 🎧 1–21 **Listen.** Circle the correct answers.

1. The uniform style of Christ's Hospital is
   (**new / old**).

2. To show their good performance in
   school, students wear (**silver buttons /
   colorful socks**).

3. The most famous part of the uniform is the
   (**neck band / blue coat**).

4. Students of Christ's Hospital (**want /
   don't want**) to change their uniform.

Discussion. What do you think of the Christ's Hospital uniform? What kind of school uniform
would you like to wear?

Pronunciation
Consonant blends with *s*

A 🎧 1-22 **Listen and repeat.**

1. small   2. sneakers   3. sweater

4. skirt   5. sleeve   6. style

B 🎧 1-23 **Listen.** Circle the sounds you hear.

1. sk   sm   2. sl   sm   3. sn   st   4. sn   sk   5. st   sl   6. sw   sk

C **Work with a partner.** Take turns to read the words below.

1. smart   2. slow   3. street   4. snake   5. sky   6. swim

> **IDIOM**
>
> To "put yourself in his shoes" means to _____ .
> a. tell him your ideas
> b. imagine his situation
> c. wear his clothes

Communication

Play a game. For each item, find someone who bought it recently. Write the name of the person and ask when he or she bought it.

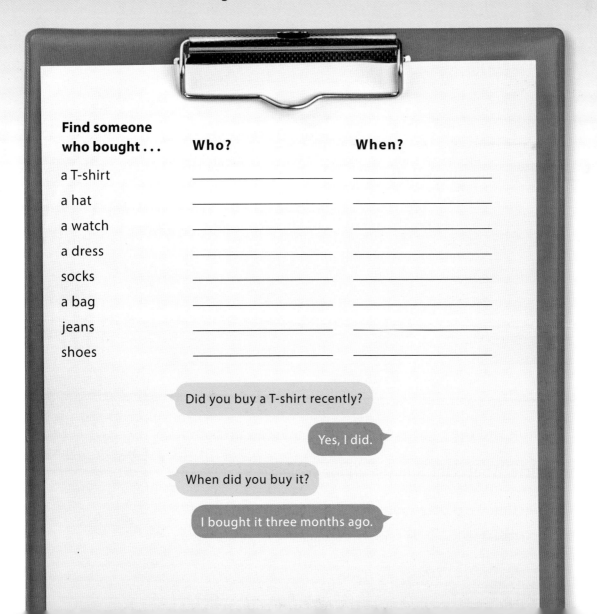

Find someone who bought . . .	Who?	When?
a T-shirt		
a hat		
a watch		
a dress		
socks		
a bag		
jeans		
shoes		

Did you buy a T-shirt recently?

Yes, I did.

When did you buy it?

I bought it three months ago.

Reading

A **Look at the title and the photos.** What do you think a yarn bomb is?

B **Skim the article.** What is the Knit the Bridge project?

C **Talk with a partner.** Why do you think people yarn bomb?

**A bridge in Pittsburgh
covered in a yarn bomb**

Benches covered in a colorful yarn bomb in San Francisco

YARN BOMB!

🎧 1–24

When most people think of knitting, they think of sweaters, scarves, or hats made from yarn. Yarn is a thin piece of cotton or wool. But some people do something different with knitting. They yarn bomb! Yarn bombing is a kind of street art. People knit colorful "jackets" to
5 cover large objects, such as cars, trees, bicycles, and even bridges!

Knit the Bridge is the largest yarn bomb project ever in the United States. Hundreds of people knitted 2,500 panels and covered the Andy Warhol Bridge in Pittsburgh with them. The project brought together two things the city is famous for—bridges and arts. It was a
10 special project because many different groups of people—schools, churches, and museums—worked on it together. The people of Pittsburgh became closer through the project.

Yarn bombing is becoming popular around the world. You can find examples of yarn bombing in many places, such as London,
15 Copenhagen, Paris, Mexico City, and Bali. Yarn bombers hope to tell stories through their knit art. They want to make their cities more colorful and interesting. They also want people to see their cities in a different way.

Comprehension

A Answer the questions about *Yarn Bomb!*

1. Main Idea Yarn bombers cover _____ with a knitted "jacket."

   a. public objects   b. people   c. dangerous objects

2. Detail The people of Pittsburgh yarn bombed _____ .

   a. a park   b. a bridge   c. a building

3. Reference In line 11, "it" refers to _____ .

   a. the bridge   b. Pittsburgh   c. Knit the Bridge

4. Inference People became closer through Knit the Bridge because it required _____ .

   a. money   b. teamwork   c. knitting skills

5. Detail Yarn bombers take part in yarn bombing to make their cities _____ .

   a. busier   b. cleaner   c. more interesting

DO YOU KNOW?

At first, knitting was a job for _____ only.

a. artists
b. poor people
c. men

B **Complete the chart.** Write notes about yarn bombing.

What's yarn bombing?	Where does it take place?	Why do people do it?

C **CRITICAL THINKING** **Talk with a partner.** Do you think yarn bombing is a form of art? Would you like to see yarn bombs in your city?

Writing

Write a short article. Describe a type of fashion or your favorite style.

Jeans in History

Jeans are a type of pants. Levi Strauss and Jacob Davis invented jeans in 1873. Farmers and factory workers first wore jeans. Then in the 1950s, lots of people thought boot-cut jeans were really cool. In the 1960s . . .

VIDEO

Walking in Style

ABOUT THE VIDEO

We wear different kinds of shoes to do different things.

BEFORE YOU WATCH

Match. Join the different types of shoes to their names.

1. ○   ○ a. sneakers

2. ○   ○ b. slippers

3. ○   ○ c. high heels

4. ○   ○ d. platform shoes

WHILE YOU WATCH

A **Check your answers to the Before You Watch questions.**

B **Watch the video again.** Circle **T** for True or **F** for False.

1. The shoes you wear can show your personality.	T	F
2. People first made shoes to make their feet look beautiful.	T	F
3. The most popular shoe is the sneaker.	T	F
4. Seventy percent of people wear sneakers for sports.	T	F

AFTER YOU WATCH

Talk with a partner. What's your favorite pair of shoes? Do you feel different when you wear different shoes?

WHAT'S THE
COLDEST
PLACE ON EARTH?

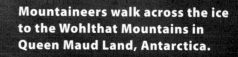
Mountaineers walk across the ice
to the Wohlthat Mountains in
Queen Maud Land, Antarctica.

Preview

A 🎧1–25 **Work with a partner.** Answer the questions. Then listen and check your answers.

1. What's the hottest desert on Earth?	The Atacama	The Sahara
2. What's the longest river in the world?	The Amazon	The Nile
3. What's the highest mountain in the world?	Mount Kilimanjaro	Mount Everest
4. What's the largest rock on Earth?	Uluru/Ayers Rock	Zuma Rock
5. Where's the coldest place on Earth?	Europe	Antarctica
6. Where's the tallest tree in the world?	The United States	Mexico
7. What's the smallest country in the world?	Vatican City	The Maldives

B 🎧1–26 **Listen.** Write the number of each place (**1–7**) on the correct continent on the map.

C **Talk with a partner.** What do you know about the places in **A**?

> The Atacama Desert is in Chile and Peru.

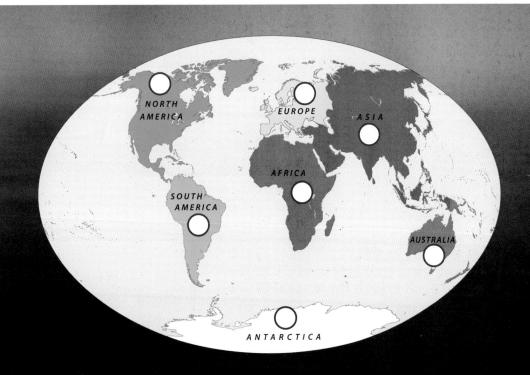

Language Focus

A 🎧1–27 **Listen and read.** Then repeat the conversation and replace the words in blue.

REAL ENGLISH Don't worry about it.

B **Practice with a partner.** Replace any words to make your own conversation.

1

Let's watch a movie after school!

I can't. I've got a **geography** test. It's my **most difficult** class.

science / hardest
social studies / worst

2

Let me help! Let's see. What's the **coldest continent** in the world?

Oh, don't worry about it. I . . .

biggest insect
oldest culture

3

OK, so what's the world's **highest mountain**?

But Maya, this isn't the hard part.

most dangerous plant
most common language

4

What's the hard part, then?

Finding a quiet place to study!

🎧1–28

DESCRIBING EXTREMES		
What's **the longest** river in the world?	The Nile is **the longest** river in the world.	big → the bi**gg**est
		pretty → the pretti**est**
		famous → the **most** famous
What's **the tiniest** dog?	**The tiniest** dog is the Chihuahua.	good → the **best**
		bad → the **worst**
Some people think that Hyams Beach in Australia has **the most beautiful** sand in the world.		less → the **least**

C **Complete the sentences.** Use the correct forms of the words in parentheses.

1. Vatican City is _____ (**small**) country in the world. It's only 0.44 km^2 and has only 840 people.

2. Some of _____ (**bad**) storms in the world happen in India.

3. Some people think that Atenas, Costa Rica, has _____ (**good**) weather In the world.

4. Many say that Paris is _____ (**beautiful**) city in the world.

5. In 2014, Misao Okawa from Japan was _____ (**old**) living person. She was 116 years old!

6. The anaconda is _____ (**large**) snake in the world.

D 🎧1–29 **Complete the sentences.** Use the correct forms of the words in the box. Then listen and check your answers.

| small   heavy   dangerous   fast |

1. The blue whale is _____ animal in the world.

2. The inland taipan is _____ snake in the world.

3. The falcon is _____ bird in the world.

4. The pygmy marmoset is _____ monkey in the world.

E **Work in a group.** Use the words in the box to talk about things you know about.

most	least	long	short	high	low
big	small	hot	cold	dry	wet

The highest mountain in my country is Mount Fuji.

The most expensive restaurant in my city is a French restaurant.

The Real World

Going to Extremes

Explorer Nick Middleton teaches geography at Oxford University in England. But he also explores extreme places— the hottest, coldest, wettest, and driest spots on Earth—to find out how people live in these places.

In an interview with National Geographic, Middleton talks about his trip to Oymyakon, in Siberia, Russia—the coldest inhabited place on Earth. It can get as cold as −71°C there!

A **Read the information about Nick Middleton.** What are his jobs?

a. explorer and scientist

b. writer and photographer

c. teacher and explorer

B 🎧 1–30 **Listen.** Check (✓) the things people usually eat in Oymyakon.

◯ reindeer meat   ◯ rice

◯ horsemeat   ◯ bread

C 🎧 1–30 **Listen again.** What do they do with their animals? Check (✓) the correct answer(s).

◯ eat them   ◯ sell them

◯ drink their milk   ◯ use them for farming

◯ make things from their leather and fur

Discussion. Would you like to live in Oymyakon? Why or why not?

Pronunciation
Sentence stress

A 🎧1-31 **Listen and repeat.**

1. The Sahara is the biggest desert in Africa.

2. What's the happiest country in Asia?

3. Redwoods are the tallest trees on Earth.

4. What's the windiest place in North America?

B 🎧1-32 **Read the sentences below.** Underline the important words. Then listen and circle the stressed words.

1. (Antarctica) is the (coldest) (place) on (Earth).

2. What's the most famous city in Europe?

3. The Nile is the longest river in the world.

4. Mount Everest is the tallest mountain on Earth.

5. Where's the tallest waterfall in South America?

6. The Amazon is the largest river in the world.

C **Work with a partner.** Take turns to read the sentences in **B.**

DO YOU KNOW?

Antarctica is the driest place on Earth. It has _____ of the Earth's water, but it's in the form of ice.

a. 50%

b. 70%

c. 90%

Communication

Play a quiz game. Work with a partner. **Student A:** Turn to page 131. **Student B:** Turn to page 132. Take turns to ask and answer questions.

> What's the largest island in the world? Madagascar or Greenland?

> Is it Greenland?

> Yes! You're right!

A herd of hippos relaxing in the Nile

Brazilian researchers working
in the Amazon rain forest

Reading

A **Scan the article.** Where does the Amazon River begin and end?

B **Skim the article.** Find two examples of why the Amazon is "extreme."

C **CRITICAL THINKING** **Talk with a partner.** Do you think the Amazon
is important to us? Why?

The anaconda is the world's largest snake.

EXTREME AMAZON!

🎧 1–33

Twenty percent of all the water that goes into oceans around the world comes from one river—the Amazon.

The Amazon River begins in the Andes Mountains in Peru. It travels about 6,000 kilometers to the Atlantic Ocean. It is the largest river in
5 the world. It is also the second longest. Most of the Amazon's water comes from rain. During the rainy season, parts of the river are 190 kilometers wide.

The Amazon River goes through the world's largest rain forest. The Amazon rain forest is home to the highest number of plant and
10 animal species on Earth. There are 2.5 million kinds of insects, such as the world's largest ant. At least 3,000 kinds of fish live there, and one-fifth of all the bird species in the world.

Some of the Amazon's animals are dangerous, such as the anaconda, the largest snake in the world. But there are also gentle animals, like
15 the sloth and the pink dolphin.

The Amazon is very important to Earth. There are still many kinds of animals and plants there that we don't know about. If we lose the Amazon, we will lose a big part of life on Earth.

Comprehension

A Answer the questions about *Extreme Amazon!*

1. `Main Idea` The article is mainly about the Amazon's _____.

   a. people   b. weather   c. importance

2. `Detail` The Amazon River is _____ long.

   a. 3,000 km   b. 6,000 km   c. 2.5 million km

3. `Inference` The Amazon River is narrower during the _____ season.

   a. dry   b. cold   c. rainy

4. `Vocabulary` In line 10, the word "species" means _____.

   a. colors   b. types   c. sizes

5. `Detail` _____ of all the bird species in the world live in the Amazon rain forest.

   a. Half   b. One-third   c. One-fifth

B Complete the word web.

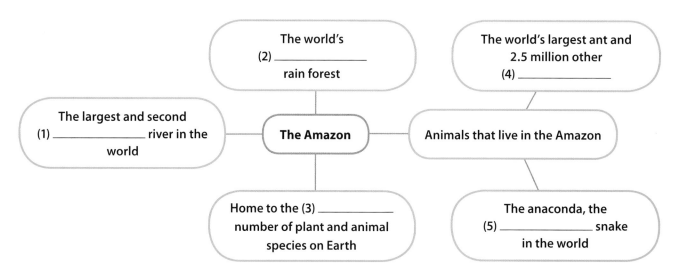

The world's
(2) _____
rain forest

The world's largest ant and
2.5 million other
(4) _____

The largest and second
(1) _____ river in the
world

The Amazon

Animals that live in the Amazon

Home to the (3) _____
number of plant and animal
species on Earth

The anaconda, the
(5) _____ snake
in the world

C Talk with a partner. What other rain forests do you know about? Describe them.

Writing

Make a poster. Describe an extreme place.

Extreme Chile!

Chile is the longest country in the world. It is 4,630 kilometers long from north to south. The driest desert in the world, the Atacama Desert, is in Chile. In some places in the Atacama, there is no rain. Plants and animals cannot live in these areas.

Earth's Coldest Place

ABOUT THE VIDEO

Some animals live in the coldest place on Earth.

BEFORE YOU WATCH

Circle the correct answers. What do you know about emperor penguins?

1. They look for food (**in the sea / on land**).

2. They (**can / can't**) fly.

3. They live (**alone / in groups**).

WHILE YOU WATCH

A **Check your answers to the Before You Watch questions.**

B **Watch the video again.** Answer these questions.

1. The coldest temperature in Antarctica is _____.

   a. −18°C   b. −80°C

2. Emperor penguins are the _____ of all penguins.

   a. tallest   b. smallest

3. Emperor penguins have _____ chick(s) every year.

   a. one   b. two

4. Leopard seals _____ emperor penguins.

   a. live with   b. eat

AFTER YOU WATCH

Talk with a partner. How can emperor penguins live in such a cold place? What will happen if Antarctica gets warmer?

Emperor penguins on the ice in Antarctica

ARE CATS **BETTER PETS** THAN DOGS?

Preview

A **Read the unit title.** Do you think cats or dogs are better pets? Why?

B **Do a quiz.** Check (✓) the sentences you agree with. Are you a cat or a dog person?

1. Watching a movie at home is more fun than going out. ☐

2. I trust myself more than other people. ☐

3. Having a few close friends is better than having many friends. ☐

4. My room is cleaner than most of my friends' rooms. ☐

5. The future is more important than now. ☐

> **Results:**
> *Fewer than 3 checks: You're a dog person!*
> *3 or more checks: You're a cat person!*

C **Work with a partner.** Talk about your results in **B**. Do you agree with your results? What do you think cat people or dog people are like?

I think cat people are independent.

I think dog people are playful.

Language Focus

Listen and read. Then repeat the conversation and replace the words in blue.

REAL ENGLISH Actually

B **Practice with a partner.** Replace any words to make your own conversation.

1
I really want a **dog**.

Yeah, I love **dogs**.

cat / cats
pet parrot / parrots

2
Do you have a pet, Stig?

Actually, I do. He's really **cute**. Do you want to see him?

Sure!

playful
intelligent

3
He has a funny dog face, but he's **cuter** than a dog.

Cuter than a dog?

gentler
friendlier

4
But . . . that's not a dog, it's a fish!

It's **better** than a fish, it's a dogface pufferfish!

more beautiful
more interesting

🎧 1–35

MAKING COMPARISONS		
Horses are **faster than** dogs. Hamsters are **smaller than** rabbits. I think cats are **more interesting than** fish.		
Which are **more playful**, rabbits or turtles?	Rabbits are **more playful than** turtles, but turtles are **friendlier than** rabbits. **Both** rabbits **and** turtles are playful.	big → bi**gg**er friend**ly** → friend**li**er intelligent → **more** intelligent good → **better** bad → **worse**

C Answer the questions.

1. Which are cuter, rabbits or mice? <u>Rabbits are cuter than mice</u> .

2. Which are stronger, elephants or rhinos? _____ .

3. Which are more intelligent, horses or dogs? _____ .

4. Which are worse pets, fish or lizards? _____ .

D 🎧 1-36 **Complete the conversation.** Then listen and check your answers.

Grace: Hey Sam, I heard you have a new pet. What is it?

Sam: It's a rabbit.

Grace: You have a cat, too, right? (1) _____ (**playful**), your rabbit or your cat?

Sam: My rabbit is (2) _____ (**playful**) my cat. It likes to follow me around.

Grace: My neighbor has a new pet lizard. He says it's (3) _____ (**interesting**) a pet dog.

Sam: That's cool. I heard some people have spiders and snakes for pets.

Grace: Wow! (4) _____ (**scary**), spiders or snakes?

Sam: I think snakes are (5) _____ (**scary**) spiders. I don't want a snake for a pet. I still like my rabbit and cat best. They're great.

E **Play animal bingo.** Work with a partner. Choose nine animals from the box below and place them in a 3 × 3 chart. Don't show your chart to your partner. Take turns to ask your partner questions. Ask questions by picking any two animals from your chart and comparing them. Draw a line through the animal that your partner says.

fish	cat	shark	elephant	spider
lizard	dog	monkey	snake	bird

Which are more dangerous, sharks or snakes?

I think snakes are more dangerous.

fish	monkey	bird
cat	elephant	spider
shark	dog	~~snake~~

Talking to Animals

Dogs are intelligent animals. We can teach them to do many things. Willow, an English terrier, can understand commands in a special way.

A Look at the photo. What do you think is special about Willow?

a. She can read.

b. She can write.

c. She understands different languages.

B 🎧 1–37 **Listen.** Number the sentences in order (**1–5**).

Howells wrote instructions on paper.	
Howells and Willow went to Mexico.	
Willow followed Howells' spoken instructions.	
Howells' friend asked her to teach Willow to read.	
Howells showed the paper to Willow and said the instruction.	

CRITICAL THINKING Do you think Willow is intelligent? What can we teach other animals to do?

Pronunciation
Reduction: *than*

A 🎧1-38 **Listen and repeat.**

1. Dogs are friendlier than cats.
2. A pet rabbit is more fun than a pet lizard.
3. Is a cat cuter than a dog?

B 🎧1-39 **Listen. Complete the sentences and questions.**

1. Cats are more independent _____ .
2. Tortoises are slower _____ .
3. Are dogs cuter _____ ?
4. Fish are quieter _____ .
5. Spiders are scarier _____ .

C **Work with a partner.** Take turns to read the sentences in **B**.

DO YOU KNOW?

Penguins are _____ on land than in the sea.

a. more active
b. slower
c. heavier

Communication

Make comparisons. Work in a group. Choose a word from columns **A** and **C**. Compare the animals or things using a word in column **B**. Give reasons for your comparisons. Then add your own ideas.

A	B	C
cats	interesting	video games
cell phones	fun	rabbits
chickens	noisy	guitars
lions	lazy	hamsters
parties	colorful	birds

Cats are more interesting than video games because they are playful.

I think cell phones are more fun than birds because I like to chat with people.

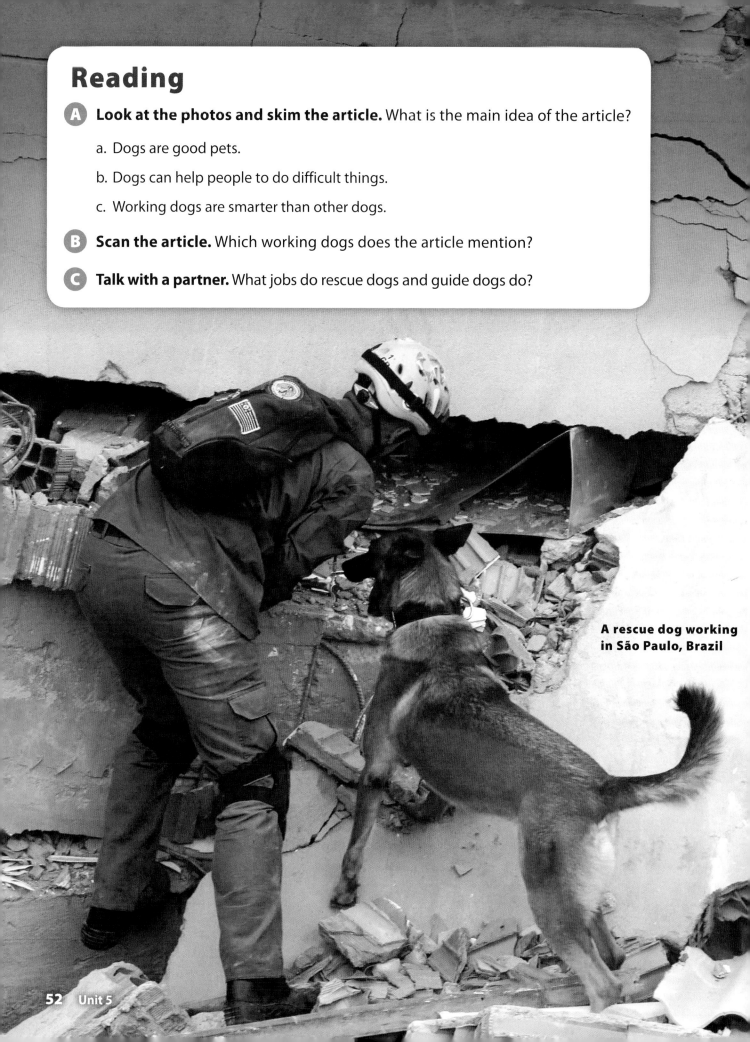

Reading

A **Look at the photos and skim the article.** What is the main idea of the article?

    a. Dogs are good pets.

    b. Dogs can help people to do difficult things.

    c. Working dogs are smarter than other dogs.

B **Scan the article.** Which working dogs does the article mention?

C **Talk with a partner.** What jobs do rescue dogs and guide dogs do?

A rescue dog working
in São Paulo, Brazil

A guide dog and her owner

DOGS with JOBS

🎧 1–40

Dogs are great pets. They're friendly, playful, and intelligent. But some dogs are smarter than others. Some of these smart dogs have special jobs—they're working dogs. Working dogs help police officers, sick people, and people who live in very cold places.

5 Rescue Dogs

Rescue dogs help people in trouble. They can find people in the mountains, in the desert, and in snow. They can even find people under buildings after an earthquake. Some common types of rescue dogs are German shepherds and Saint Bernards. These dogs are
10 stronger and more intelligent than other dogs. They have better ears and noses, too.

Guide Dogs

Guide dogs help blind people (people who cannot see). For example, they help them cross the street. Guide dogs are usually golden
15 retrievers or Labradors. These types of dogs are gentler and friendlier than other dogs. Guide dogs can help blind people have better lives.

Comprehension

A **Answer the questions about *Dogs with Jobs*.**

1. Main Idea The main idea of paragraph 1 is that working dogs are _____ than other dogs.

   a. faster   b. larger   c. more intelligent

2. Inference In line 6, "people in trouble" means people who are _____.

   a. sick   b. lost   c. lonely

3. Detail It's important for rescue dogs to _____.

   a. be friendly   b. have good eyes   c. have good ears and noses

4. Detail Which of these dogs is the best guide dog?

   a. Labradors   b. Saint Bernards   c. German shepherds

5. Inference It's important for guide dogs to be gentle because they work closely with _____.

   a. other dogs   b. animal trainers   c. people

IDIOM

"A bird in the hand is worth two in the bush" means keeping what you have now is _____ than trying to get more.
a. better
b. worse
c. more difficult

B **Complete the chart.** How are working dogs different from other dogs? Use the words in the article.

Rescue dogs ... than other dogs.	Guide dogs ... than other dogs.
are stronger	

C **CRITICAL THINKING** **Talk with a partner.** Do you think working dogs are helpful to us? What other jobs can dogs do?

Writing

Write a blog post. Describe your favorite pet or animal. Give reasons why it is better than other animals.

Home   BLOG   Photos   Contact   About Me

Iguanas are the best pets!

Iguanas are great pets because they are special. Many people have dogs and cats, but not iguanas! You don't need to take iguanas for walks. They're cleaner than rabbits because they don't have fur. They're also quieter than parrots. Parrots are noisy! My iguana is . . .

VIDEO

Strange Cats

BEFORE YOU WATCH

Circle the correct answers. What do you know about taking care of pet cats?

1. It's a (**good** / **bad**) idea to feed your cat in the same place every day.

2. It's a (**good** / **bad**) idea to give your cat toys to play with.

3. It's a (**good** / **bad**) idea to keep your cat in a small room.

WHILE YOU WATCH

A Check your answers to the Before You Watch questions.

B Watch the video again. Match the names from the video to the descriptions.

1. Steve ○   ○ a. a bored cat

2. Ricky ○   ○ b. a pet expert

3. Boo ○   ○ c. an animal doctor

4. Vint ○   ○ d. Steve's cat

AFTER YOU WATCH

Talk with a partner. Do you have a cat? How does it behave? How are house cats similar to wild cats?

I REALLY LIKE
ELECTRONIC
MUSIC!

Preview

A **Look at the photo.** How often do you go to concerts?

B 🎧1-41 **Listen.** Match the type of music to the singer or group.

1. hip-hop ○   ○ a. Daft Punk

2. rap ○   ○ b. Kanye West

3. pop ○   ○ c. Linkin Park

4. classical ○   ○ d. Pharrell Williams

5. rock ○   ○ e. Katy Perry

6. electronic ○   ○ f. Beethoven

C **Talk with a partner.** Ask about his or her favorite singers and types of music.

> Which do you like better, rock or electronic music?

> I like rock better.

Nile Rodgers and Pharrell Williams performing with Daft Punk

RECORDING

Language Focus

A 🎧1–42 **Listen and read.** Then repeat the conversation and replace the words in blue.

REAL ENGLISH   Not exactly.

B **Practice with a partner.** Replace any words to make your own conversation.

🎧1–43

EXPRESSING OPINIONS		
Do you like Daft Punk? Do you like rap?	Yes, I love **them**! No, I can't stand **it**.	
What kind of music **do** you **like (the) best**?	I really **like** hip-hop. / I **like** rap **(the) best**.	type of music → it group → them singer → him/her
Which do you **like better**, pop **or** rock? **Who** do you **like better**, Shakira **or** Jennifer Lopez?	I **like** rock **better**. I **like** Shakira **better**.	

C 🎧 1-44 **Listen.** Complete the chart by coloring in the stars.

	HIP-HOP	RAP	CLASSICAL	POP
Ana	☆☆☆☆	☆☆☆☆	☆☆☆☆	☆☆☆☆
Carl	☆☆☆☆	☆☆☆☆	☆☆☆☆	☆☆☆☆
Yoko	☆☆☆☆	☆☆☆☆	☆☆☆☆	☆☆☆☆

★ ★ ★ ★ I love it.
★ ★ ★ ☆ I like it.
★ ★ ☆ ☆ It's OK.
★ ☆ ☆ ☆ I don't like it.
☆ ☆ ☆ ☆ I can't stand it.

D 🎧 1-44 **Listen again.** Answer the questions. Use the information in **C**.

1. Does Ana like classical music? _No, she doesn't_ .

2. Does Ana like pop? _____ .

3. Does Carl like hip-hop? _____ .

4. Which does Carl like better, classical or pop? _____ .

5. Does Yoko like rap? _____ .

6. What music does Yoko like best? _____ .

E **Work with a partner.** Complete the conversation with things that are true for you. Then take turns to role-play the conversation. Repeat with different types of music and singers.

Meg: Sorry, Chris, but can you change the music? I can't stand it.

Chris: Sure. I have other kinds of music. Which do you like better,
(1) _____ or (2) _____ ? (*type of music*)

Meg: Sorry, I don't really like either of them.

Chris: Okay, what kind of music do you like best?

Meg: I guess I like pop best.

Chris: Then how about (3) _____ ? (*singer/band*)
Do you like (4) _____ ? (*him/her/them*)

Meg: Oh, I love (5) _____ ! (*him/her/them*)

Your Brain on
Music

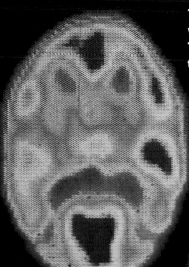

The level of brain activity when we do different tasks: The red and yellow areas are the active parts of the brain.

Does music make you cry or feel happy? Most people agree on what music sounds "happy" and what sounds "sad." But no one really understands why music makes us feel different emotions.

Researchers say that music makes our brain active. It makes our brain "feel happy." This explains the importance of music in cultures all over the world.

Listening to music

Resting

A 🎧 1–45 **Listen to the music.** Check (✓) the feeling you think each piece represents. Then compare results as a class.

	HAPPY	SAD	SCARED
1.			
2.			
3.			
4.			

B **Do an experiment.** As a class, create a list of ten random words. Then get into two groups.

Group 1: Remember the words on the list by reading them.

Group 2: Remember the words on the list by singing them. Use any song you know.

Cover the list and say the words in order. Count the number of words people in each group remembered correctly.

Discussion. Was there a difference in the results of the two groups? Why or why not?

Pronunciation

Syllable stress

A 🎧1–46 **Listen.** Write the number of syllables. Then listen again and repeat.

1. popular _3_ 2. amazing ____ 3. independent ____

B 🎧1–47 **Listen.** Write the number of syllables. Then listen again and underline the stressed syllable.

1. interesting ____ 4. different ____

2. terrible ____ 5. important ____

3. intelligent ____ 6. dangerous ____

C **Work with a partner.** Make sentences using the words in **B**. Then take turns to read the sentences.

IDIOM

"That's music to my ears"
means ____ .

a. I can hear music
b. I like what you said
c. your voice is musical

Communication

Take a poll. Ask your classmates to rate each kind of music using the chart below. Find out the most popular kind of music in your class. Then turn to page 131 and follow the instructions.

KINDS OF MUSIC	NAME:	NAME:	NAME:	NAME:	TOTAL POINTS
hip-hop					
pop					
rap					
rock					
electronic					
classical					

Do you like hip-hop?

I don't really like it.

What about pop?

I love it!

0: I can't stand it.

1: I don't really like it.

2: It's all right/OK.

3: I like it.

4: I love it.

Reading

A **Look at the title and the photo.** What do you think the article is about?

   a. a concert

   b. a famous musician

   c. a special musical instrument

B **Talk with a partner.** What do you think the title means?

C **Talk with a partner.** Do you play any musical instruments? What musical instruments do you want to learn to play?

THE FEEL of MUSIC

🎧 1–48

One of the world's most famous musicians "hears" through her feet. Evelyn Glennie is profoundly deaf—she has very serious hearing loss. She plays music by feeling the movement that sounds make.

As a child, Glennie learned to play musical instruments such as the
5 harmonica and the clarinet. She was also a good piano student. But when she was eight, she started to have hearing problems. That did not stop Glennie's love for music. She found another way of playing music. She realized that she could "hear" notes in her feet and body.

At age 12, after she saw a friend play the drums, Glennie decided to
10 take drum lessons. She studied at England's well-known Royal Academy of Music at 16. She graduated in three years. At 23, she won her first Grammy. She is the first person in musical history to have a career as a solo percussionist. Glennie now plays more than 100 concerts a year. She practices and performs with no shoes on.

15 Glennie performs with world-famous musicians like the Kodo Japanese drummers, Björk, and orchestras in the United States and Europe. She is also a keen collector of percussion instruments and owns more than 1,800 drums and other instruments.

Evelyn Glennie performing at a classical concert in Scotland

Comprehension

A **Answer the questions about** *The Feel of Music.*

1. [Detail] Glennie is a special musician because she _____.

   a. can't hear   b. never studied music   c. can play many instruments

2. [Detail] Glennie _____ music when she lost her hearing.

   a. stopped playing   b. didn't give up   c. decided to learn

3. [Inference] Glennie doesn't wear shoes when she performs so that she _____.

   a. can move quickly   b. feels relaxed   c. can "hear" the music

4. [Vocabulary] In line 17, "she is a keen collector" means that she _____ musical instruments.

   a. loves to collect   b. likes to play   c. is good at collecting

5. [Inference] Which one of these is not a percussion instrument?

   a. triangle   b. violin   c. drum

B **Complete the timeline.** Write the letters of the events below.

a. studies at the Royal Academy of Music   d. performs with famous musicians
b. wins her first Grammy   e. starts to take drum lessons
c. starts to have hearing problems   f. discovers she can "hear" notes in her body

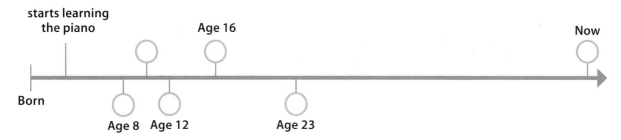

C CRITICAL THINKING **Talk with a partner.** Evelyn Glennie says listening to music with only your ears is like trying to understand a person with only your eyes. What do you think this means?

Writing

Write a music review.
Write about a new song or album you have heard, or a concert or performance you have seen.

| Home | BLOG | Photos | Contact | About Me |

The London Olympics Opening Ceremony

I watched Evelyn Glennie's performance at the London Olympics Opening Ceremony and I loved it. The music performance told a story about the lives of people in the United Kingdom. Glennie played the drums together with 1,000 other drummers! It was interesting because the drummers used buckets as drums.

The Steel Band

ABOUT THE VIDEO

The music of Trinidad and Tobago is very special.

BEFORE YOU WATCH

Look at the photo. What do you know about the steel pan? Circle **T** for True or **F** for false.

1. The steel pan was invented in the 19th century.   **T**   **F**

2. The steel pan was invented in the Caribbean.   **T**   **F**

3. Steel bands play many different kinds of music.   **T**   **F**

WHILE YOU WATCH

A **Check your answers to the Before You Watch questions.**

B **Watch the video again.** Complete the quotes.

"Pan is most important to Trinidad and Tobago because it's part of our (1) _____. It was (2) _____ in Trinidad and Tobago."

"This is ours, we made it, we (3) _____ it, it belongs to us, and we are so (4) _____ of it. We feel we can (5) _____ it with the world."

AFTER YOU WATCH

Talk with a partner. What musical instrument is popular in your country? Do you know any interesting musical instruments?

A man plays the steel pan.

Review Game 1

Play with 2–4 classmates. Take turns.
Each classmate has a game counter.
Toss a coin and move your counter.

Heads = move two squares
Tails = move one square

Can't answer? Miss a turn!

START!

1. Name four things you often eat.

2. What kind of music do you like best?

3. Explain the meaning of "that's music to my ears."

4. What clothes did you buy recently?

5. What's the driest place on Earth?

6. Explain the meaning of "to keep a straight face."

7. Which are cuter, cats or dogs?

8. Which is bigger, a soccer ball or a baseball?

9. Describe what this person is wearing.

10. What does your best friend look like?

11. Name three types of music you like.

12. What are you going to do this weekend?

13. Name the most beautiful place in your city.

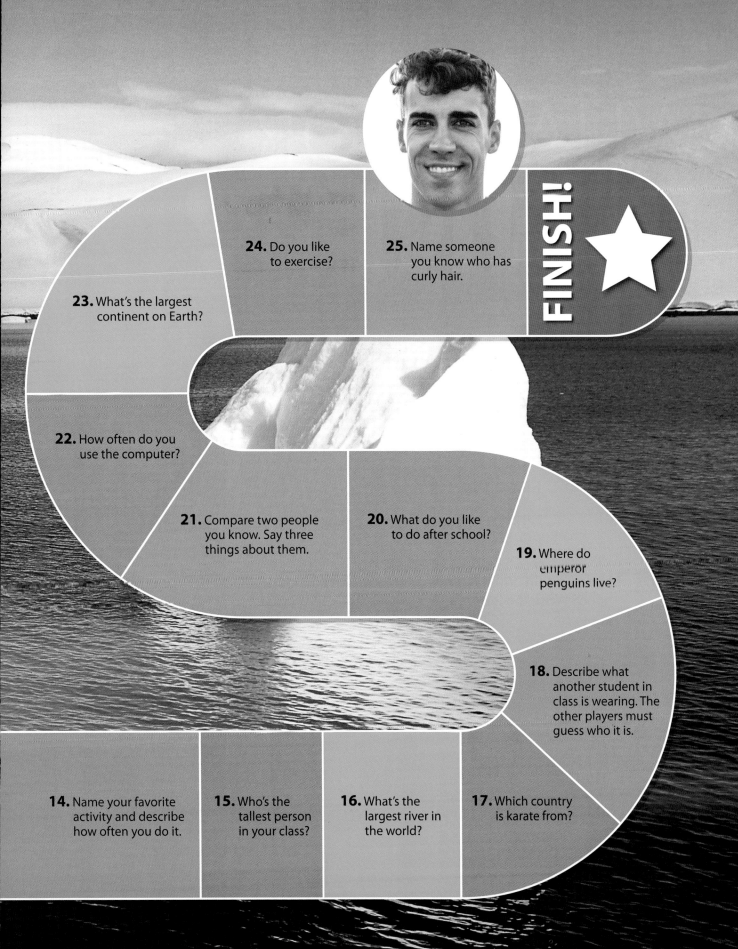

FINISH!

23. What's the largest continent on Earth?

24. Do you like to exercise?

25. Name someone you know who has curly hair.

22. How often do you use the computer?

21. Compare two people you know. Say three things about them.

20. What do you like to do after school?

19. Where do emperor penguins live?

18. Describe what another student in class is wearing. The other players must guess who it is.

14. Name your favorite activity and describe how often you do it.

15. Who's the tallest person in your class?

16. What's the largest river in the world?

17. Which country is karate from?

WHAT'S FOR DINNER?

Preview

A 🎧 2-01 **Listen.** Check (✓) the things that the people are eating or drinking.

1. Joseph ⬡ chicken ⬡ salad ⬡ noodles
2. Teresa ⬡ fish ⬡ burger ⬡ rice
3. Yuri ⬡ noodles ⬡ chicken ⬡ vegetables
4. Andrew ⬡ fruit ⬡ pasta ⬡ juice

B 🎧 2-01 **Listen again.** What kitchen item does each person need? Write the letters **J**, **T**, **Y**, or **A** below. Two items are extra.

⬤ plate �bowl ▯ glass

| spoon 🍴 fork 🔪 knife

C **Talk with a partner.** What did you eat today?

What did you have for lunch today?

I had pasta and a salad. How about you?

A family sharing a meal at
a restaurant in Hong Kong

Language Focus

A 🎧2–02 **Listen and read.** Then repeat the conversation and replace the words in blue.

B **Practice with a partner.** Replace any words to make your own conversation.

🎧2–03

DESCRIBING QUANTITY

There are some plates on the table.		There's some juice on the counter.	
There aren't any forks.		There isn't any ice cream in the refrigerator.	
Are there any apples?	Yes, there are. No, there aren't.	Is there any salad?	Yes, there is. No, there isn't.

C **Look at the photo.** Complete the sentences.

1. <u>There aren't any</u> bowls on the table.

2. _____ plates in the sink.

3. _____ soda on the counter.

4. _____ glasses in the sink.

5. _____ knives on the table.

6. _____ milk in the fridge.

D **Work with a partner.** Look at the photo. Complete the questions on your own. Then take turns to ask and answer.

1. _____ milk on the counter?

2. _____ bowls in the sink?

3. _____ ?

4. _____ ?

5. _____ ?

E **Play a game.** Work in groups of four. **Student A:** Make a list of ten things in your refrigerator. **Students B, C,** and **D:** Take turns to guess what is in Student A's refrigerator. If you make three incorrect guesses, you are out of the game.

> Is there any orange juice in your fridge?

> No, there isn't.

> Are there any vegetables in your fridge?

> Yes, there are!

Food Art

Food stylists have a special job—to make food look good. They usually work with food photographers. Food stylists have ways to make food look better than it actually is. Sometimes, food stylists use things that we can't eat!

A 🎧2-04 **Listen.** Match the food items to the things food stylists use to style them.

1. drinks ○   ○ soap bubbles ○   ○ make the color nicer

2. bread ○   ○ cake icing ○   ○ it doesn't melt

3. ice cream ○   ○ lipstick ○   ○ stop it from becoming dry

4. strawberries ○   ○ car seat spray ○   ○ make it look like someone just poured it

B 🎧2-04 **Listen again.** Match the things food stylists use to the reasons.

CRITICAL THINKING Where can you find photos of styled food?

Pronunciation

Linked sounds

A 🎧2-05 **Listen and repeat.**

1. There are spoons in the cabinet.
2. There are forks on the table.
3. Are there any cookies in the bowl?
4. Are there any snacks on the counter?

B 🎧2-06 **Listen.** Complete the sentences.

1. There are some _____ the sink.
2. Are there any _____ the table?
3. There are some _____ the counter.
4. Are there any _____ the plate?
5. There are some _____ the cabinet.
6. Are there any _____ the table?

C **Work with a partner.** Take turns to read the sentences in **B**.

DO YOU KNOW?

You can't taste the difference between apples and potatoes if you _____ while eating them.

a. close your eyes
b. raise your hand
c. pinch your nose

Communication

Find the differences. Work with a partner. **Student A:** Look at the photo below.
Student B: Look at the photo on page 134. Take turns asking and answering questions to find six differences. Circle them.

Is there any bread? Where is it?

Yes, there is. It's on a plate.

A man making
pizza

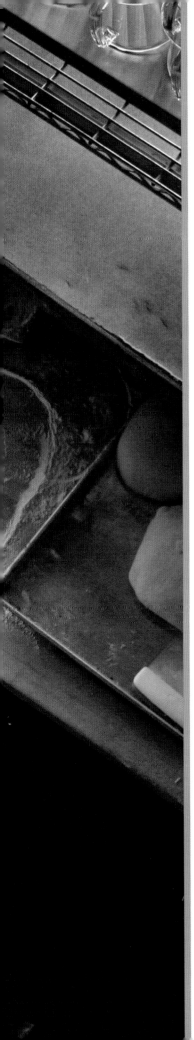

Reading

A **Look at the photo and read the headings.** What is the article about?

    a. the ingredients in pizza

    b. how people started making pizza

    c. how to make pizza

B **Skim the article.** How did people make the first pizza?

C **Scan the article.** Where was the first pizzeria (pizza restaurant)?

A SLICE OF
HISTORY

🎧 2–07

What's your favorite pizza? Cheese? Meat? Veggie? Many people around the world love pizza. But where did it come from?

The First Pizza. Every pizza has a crust. A crust is a thin, flat bread. Five to ten thousand years ago, people made this kind of bread on hot rocks.
5 Some people put other food on top of the bread. This was the world's first pizza.

Food for Soldiers. About 2,500 years ago, the Persian army was a long way from home. The soldiers did not have any ovens, but they cooked pizza crust on their metal shields. They put some cheese and
10 other things on it.

Dangerous Tomatoes? Explorers from South America brought tomatoes to Europe in the 1520s. At first, the Europeans thought tomatoes were poisonous. But people soon found out that tomatoes were OK to eat. Today, tomato sauce is a basic topping on pizza.

15 **The First Pizzeria.** Pizza makers opened the world's first pizza restaurant, or pizzeria, in 1830, in Naples, Italy. They used hot lava from a volcano to cook the pizza!

Pizza for the World. In the late 19th century, many Italians moved to the United States. Some of them opened pizzerias, and pizza became
20 very popular. Now, pizza is sold all over the world. People eat about 5 billion pizzas every year!

Comprehension

A **Answer the questions about *A Slice of History*.**

1. Detail People used _____ to make pizza crust five thousand years ago.

   a. hot rocks   b. ovens   c. shields

2. Reference In line 10, "it" refers to _____.

   a. a pizza crust   b. cheese   c. a shield

3. Vocabulary In line 13, the word "poisonous" means _____ to eat.

   a. popular   b. dangerous   c. healthy

4. Detail The first pizzeria is about _____ years old.

   a. 2,500   b. 1,830   c. 200

5. Main Idea The last paragraph of the article is about how pizza _____ around the world.

   a. is made   b. is different   c. became popular

> **IDIOM**
>
> **"Your eyes are bigger than your stomach" means _____ .**
>
> a. you like looking at food
> b. you can't finish your food
> c. you eat a lot

B **Complete the timeline.** Write notes about the history of pizza.

History of Pizza

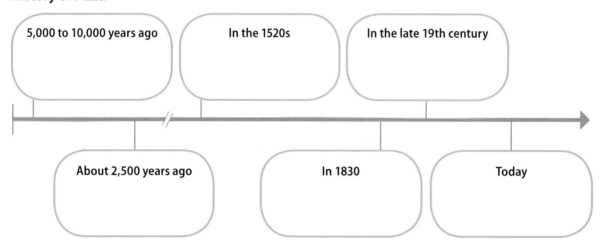

5,000 to 10,000 years ago	In the 1520s	In the late 19th century

About 2,500 years ago	In 1830	Today

C **Talk with a partner.** Think of a popular dish from your country. What are its ingredients? When did people start making it?

Writing

Write a text message. Imagine you are preparing for a barbecue. Ask your friend or family member for help in buying some things that you need.

Messages

Hey, Vera! Where are you now? I'm getting ready for our family barbecue, but there isn't enough food. We have some fruit, bread, and meat. But we don't have any salad or juice. Please buy some on your way here!

Send

VIDEO

The King of Fruits

ABOUT THE VIDEO

The durian has an interesting shape and a unique taste.

BEFORE YOU WATCH

Check (✓) the words you think describe a durian.

- ◯ salty
- ◯ smelly
- ◯ cheap
- ◯ hard
- ◯ spiky
- ◯ small

WHILE YOU WATCH

A Check your answers to the Before You Watch question.

B Watch the video again. Circle **T** for True or **F** for False.

1. Most durians come from Africa.	**T**	**F**
2. Durians grow on trees.	**T**	**F**
3. Some hotels in Malaysia try to stop people from bringing durians inside.	**T**	**F**
4. Hotels use a special machine to remove the durian smell.	**T**	**F**

AFTER YOU WATCH

Talk with a partner. Would you like to try durian? Is there any food in your country that has a strong smell?

The durian

YOU SHOULD SEE A
DOCTOR!

Preview

A 🎧2–08 **Listen.** Circle the body parts that Rick injured.

1. foot   2. hand   3. knee   4. leg   5. back   6. arm

B 🎧2–09 **Listen.** Circle the correct answers.

1. Anton has a (**backache** / **headache**).

2. Janet's sister (**broke** / **cut**) her leg.

3. Sonia has a (**sore** / **broken**) back.

4. Eric (**hurt** / **broke**) his knee when he fell. He (**hurt** / **cut**) his hand, too.

C **Talk with a partner.** Talk about a time you hurt yourself.

> I cut my hand yesterday when I was cooking.

> Last month, I fell on the street. I hurt my knees.

Language Focus

A 🎧 2-10 **Listen and read.** Then repeat the conversation and replace the words in blue.

REAL ENGLISH Come on!

B **Practice with a partner.** Replace any words to make your own conversation.

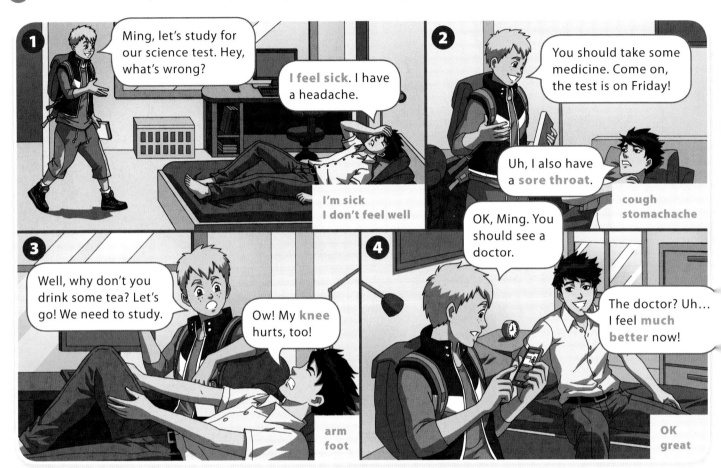

🎧 2-11

GIVING ADVICE	
Maya is sick. She has a sore throat. What **should** she **do**?	She **should** stay home and rest.
I have a cough. What **should** I **do**?	You **should** take some cough medicine. **Why don't** you take some cough medicine?
Emma and Kevin both have a cold. **Should** they go to a doctor?	Yes, they **should**. No, they **shouldn't**.

C Circle the correct answers.

1. Janice has a stomachache. She (**should** / **shouldn't**) see a doctor.

2. I hurt my foot. The doctor says I (**should** / **shouldn't**) rest for a week.

3. You look tired. (**Should** / **Why don't**) you get some rest?

4. Everyone is sleeping, so we (**should** / **shouldn't**) make a lot of noise.

5. Diego is good at drawing. (**Should** / **Why don't**) you ask him for help?

D 🎧2-12 **Complete the questions.** Write responses with *should, shouldn't*, or *why don't you*. Then listen and check your answers.

1. Jay: I (1) _____ headache. What (2) _____ I do?

   Sally: (3) _____ take some medicine?

2. Nancy: I (4) _____ backache. What (5) _____?

   Peter: (6) _____ stay home and rest?

3. Lee: Victor has a toothache. (7) _____ eat ice cream?

   Erika: No, he (8) _____.

4. Ian: Lisa (9) _____ ear ache. (10) _____
            stay home and rest?

   Wendy: Yes, she (11) _____. She (12) _____ go to work.

E **Play charades.** Work in a group. Take turns to act out a health problem. Work together to guess the problem and give two suggestions.

Do you have a cough?

Yes, I do! What should I do?

Why don't you take some medicine? You should also drink more water.

Disease Hunter

Nathan Wolfe is a National Geographic Explorer. He is an expert on diseases. He studies how diseases spread and he wants to find a way to stop pandemics before they happen.

A 🎧 2–13 **Listen.** Circle **T** for True or **F** for False.

1. A pandemic is a disease that spreads quickly to many people.	**T**	**F**
2. International travel helps to prevent pandemics.	**T**	**F**
3. Wolfe does his research mainly in Europe.	**T**	**F**
4. Many diseases start in animals and move into humans.	**T**	**F**

B 🎧 2–14 **Listen.** Check (✓) the advice you hear.

- ☐ stay healthy
- ☐ wear a mask
- ☐ go to a hospital
- ☐ keep some money at home
- ☐ stay at home and rest
- ☐ have a list of emergency numbers

CRITICAL THINKING Do you worry about disease? What diseases have you read or heard about in the news?

Pronunciation
Should, could, would

A 🎧 2-15 **Listen and repeat.**

1. should, shouldn't   2. could, couldn't   3. would, wouldn't

B 🎧 2-16 **Listen.** Write the words you hear.

1. If Danny has a backache, he _____ rest.

2. The music was too loud. I ___ ___ hear what she was saying.

3. It's raining. They _____ play soccer outdoors.

4. _____ you like some orange juice?

C **Work with a partner.** Take turns to read the sentences in **B**.

You should cover your mouth and nose when you sneeze. The air from your sneeze can travel about ____ km/h!

a. 10
b. 30
c. 60

Communication

Do a survey. Work in a group of four. First, check (✓) the healthy habits you follow. Then ask your group members about their healthy habits. Discuss the results as a group. Talk about the things you can do to stay healthy.

HEALTHY HABITS	ME	2. _____	3. _____	4. _____
1. I eat breakfast every day.				
2. I always wash my hands before I eat.				
3. I get lots of rest.				
4. I eat lots of fruits and vegetables.				
5. I get plenty of exercise.				
6. I drink lots of water.				
7. I take a walk every day.				
8. I protect my skin with sunscreen.				

Do you eat breakfast every day?

No, I don't.

You should have breakfast every day. It's a good way to start the day.

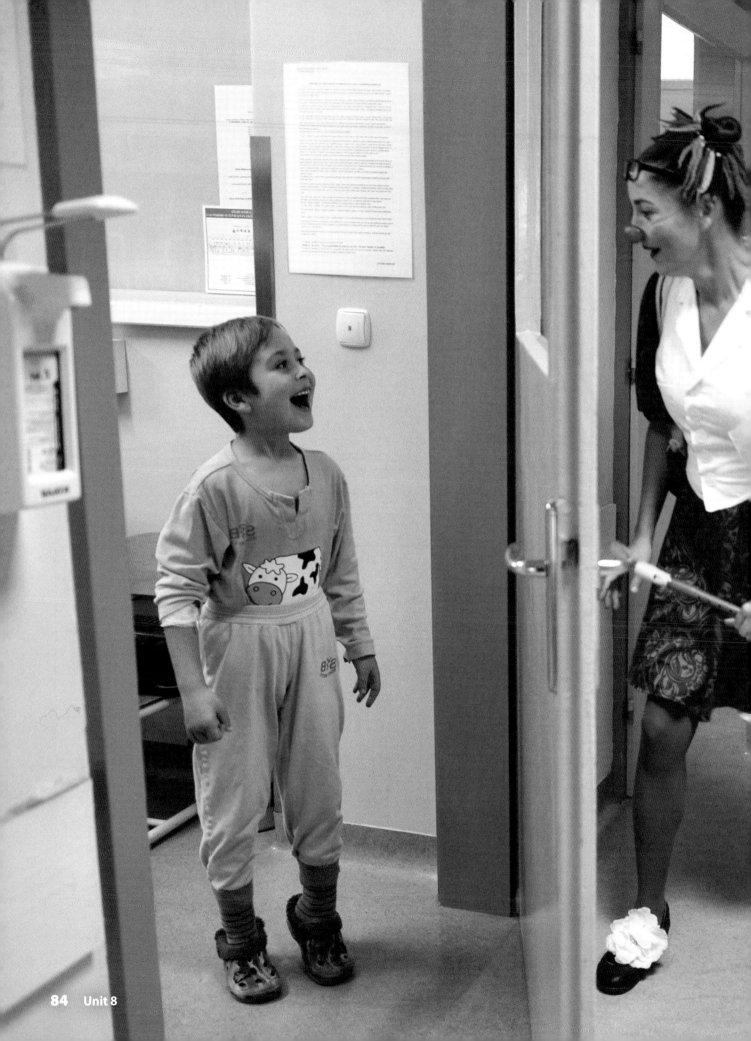

"Clown doctors" work in hospitals. These actors do magic, sing songs, and tell stories to make patients laugh.

Reading

A **Work with a partner.** Look at the photo. Why do you think clown doctors want to make patients laugh?

B **Scan the article.** Circle two words that have a similar meaning to "laugh."

C **Talk with a partner.** How is laughing good for you?

LAUGHTER IS THE BEST MEDICINE

🎧 2–17

Laugh with friends or giggle at a cartoon. It doesn't matter why you're laughing—laughter is good for you, and that's no joke!

A good laugh helps you right away. When you laugh, changes happen in your body. For example, you take in more air, which is good for your
5 heart. A good laugh increases your heart rate. When you laugh, your brain also releases chemicals that make you feel happy. Laughing can also make you feel relaxed for up to 45 minutes.

Laughter can also reduce pain. You probably don't want to chuckle when you're injured, but laughter helps the body make its own
10 natural pain medicine. Laughing is also great exercise! Research shows that laughing 100 times is as good as riding a bike for 15 minutes.

Negative thoughts can cause you to feel sad or worried. But when you laugh, your brain makes chemicals that make these feelings go
15 away. These chemicals also prevent some illnesses. Many scientists also believe laughter is good for your mental health—it helps people communicate better with each other.

So why don't you try laughing out loud every day? See how you feel. Are your muscles less tense? Do you feel more relaxed? That's
20 laughter at work.

Comprehension

A **Answer the questions about** *Laughter is the Best Medicine.*

1. Main Idea Laughter has _____ effect on our health.

   a. a powerful   b. a negative   c. no

2. Detail When you laugh, your heart beats _____ .

   a. slower   b. faster   c. at the same rate

3. Detail Laughing when you're injured _____ .

   a. reduces the pain   b. stops the pain   c. makes the injury worse

4. Vocabulary When you think negative thoughts, you imagine _____ things happening. (line 13)

   a. happy   b. bad   c. unusual

5. Inference Laughter improves communication because it makes conversations _____ .

   a. longer   b. cooler   c. friendlier

> **IDIOM**
>
> **"She laughed her head off" means she _____ .**
>
> a. laughed very loudly
> b. had a headache
> c. laughed at the wrong time

B **Work with a partner.** Changes happen in your body when you laugh. Complete the word web.

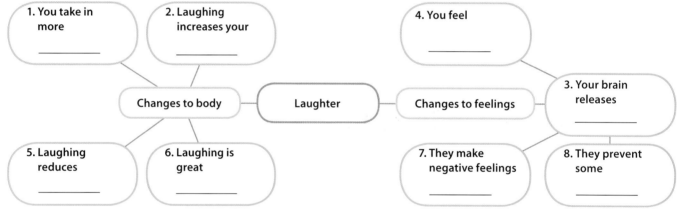

1. You take in more _____

2. Laughing increases your _____

4. You feel _____

Changes to body — Laughter — Changes to feelings

3. Your brain releases _____

5. Laughing reduces _____

6. Laughing is great _____

7. They make negative feelings _____

8. They prevent some _____

C **Talk with a partner.** Do you laugh often? What do you do when you feel sad or stressed?

Writing

Write a short article.
Describe a healthy habit you know about and give some advice.

Yoga Is Good For You

Yoga helps you to stretch your muscles and make them strong. It is good for you in many other ways, too.

Better Sleep Yoga helps you to relax your body. It slows down your breathing and lowers your heart rate. To sleep better, you should do yoga at least three times a week.

Less Stress You should practice yoga because it can help to reduce stress. We sometimes feel stressed because we think about a lot of things. Yoga helps you remove those thoughts and think only about your breathing.

Yoga is a good exercise for your body and mind. Try it!

Laughter Yoga

ABOUT THE VIDEO

The members of the Laughter Club believe that laughing can be good for you in many ways.

BEFORE YOU WATCH

Check (✓) the items that are true. Why do you think people join the Laughter Club?

◯ It makes them feel happy.

◯ It can help them lose weight.

◯ They like to share jokes.

◯ It is good exercise.

WHILE YOU WATCH

A **Check your answers to the Before You Watch question.**

B **Watch the video again.** Circle the correct answers.

1. Laughing can make your blood vessels _____.

   a. cleaner   b. wider

2. You can burn _____ calories when you laugh for five to ten minutes.

   a. 40   b. 400

3. We start laughing when we are around _____.

   a. one month old   b. three months old

AFTER YOU WATCH

Talk with a partner. Would you join a laughter club? Why or why not? Do you think laughter is better than exercise?

People of the Laughter Club doing laughter yoga

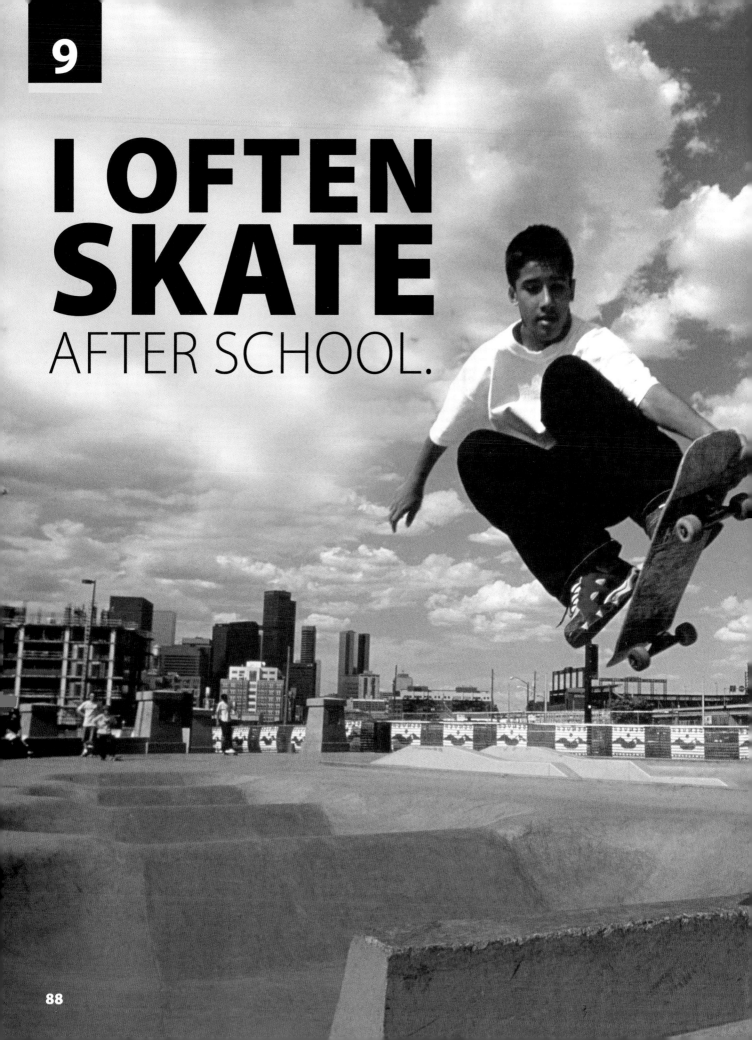

9

I OFTEN SKATE
AFTER SCHOOL.

Preview

A 🎧 2–18 **Listen.** Match the people to the activities they are doing.

1. Tim ○	○ running ○	○ after school
2. Dan ○	○ cooking ○	○ on Thursdays
3. Luis ○	○ skating ○	○ twice a week
4. Susana ○	○ studying ○	○ on Fridays
5. Ben ○	○ practicing ○ the violin	○ every day

B 🎧 2–18 **Listen again.** Match the activities to when the people do them.

C **Talk with a partner.** What do you do after school?

> I have dance practice after school on Mondays.

> I cycle at the park every week.

A teenager at a skateboard park in Colorado, U.S.A.

Language Focus

A 🎧 2–19 **Listen and read.** Then repeat the conversation and replace the words in blue.

REAL ENGLISH Just a minute.

B **Practice with a partner.** Replace any words to make your own conversation.

🎧 2–20

DESCRIBING MY ACTIVITIES

What are you **doing**? **Is** she **cleaning** her room?	I'm **reading** a magazine. Yes, she **is**. / No, she **isn't**.		
What do you usually **do** after school?	I **play** soccer		**once in a while**. **every day**.
Do you often **go** to the movies?	No, I	**seldom** **rarely** **hardly ever**	**go** to the movies.

C Circle the correct answers.

1. Don (**listens** / **is listening**) to music right now.

2. Alice (**chats** / **is chatting**) online every day.

3. Min (**studies** / **is studying**) for a test tomorrow.

4. They (**practice** / **are practicing**) the violin on Saturday mornings.

5. Mark (**plays** / **is playing**) soccer with his friends after school on Wednesdays.

D 🎧2–21 **Complete the sentences.** Use the correct forms of the words. Then listen and check your answers.

buy	drive	study
talk	make	watch

1. Rachel _____ a drink at the store on her way to school every day.

2. Karen usually walks to school, but today her mom's _____ her.

3. Normally, Henry _____ to his friends on the phone after school, but today he's reading.

4. I rarely _____ movies at the cinema. I usually buy DVDs.

5. Shh! You shouldn't _____ so much noise. People _____.

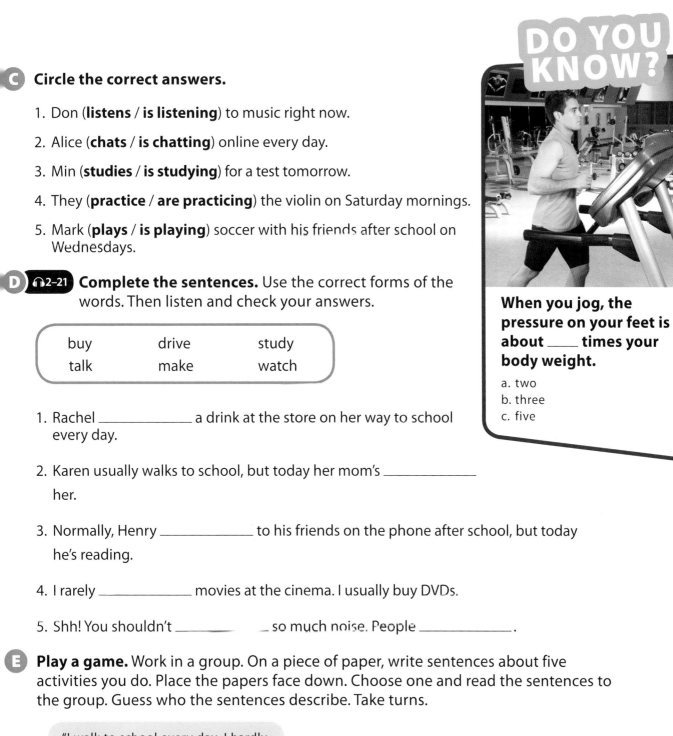

DO YOU KNOW?

When you jog, the pressure on your feet is about ____ times your body weight.

a. two
b. three
c. five

E **Play a game.** Work in a group. On a piece of paper, write sentences about five activities you do. Place the papers face down. Choose one and read the sentences to the group. Guess who the sentences describe. Take turns.

"I walk to school every day. I hardly ever play sports." Is this you, Judy?

Sorry, not me!

The Science of
Habits

People usually do things in a certain way. This is why habits are important in our lives. They help us to do our everyday activities well. But sometimes, we form bad habits, too.

A 🎧2–22 **Circle the correct answers.** Then listen and check.

1. People form habits when they (**repeat** / **see**) the same actions many times.

2. Habits make us (**think more** / **think less**) when we do certain things.

3. A "cue" is something that makes us (**do** / **stop**) a habit.

B 🎧2–23 **Listen.** Circle **T** for True or **F** for False.

1. The brain makes us want to eat sweet or salty food.   T   F

2. You feel like you're eating more when you use a bigger plate.   T   F

3. One way to eat healthier is to mix different kinds of food.   T   F

4. You should start a meal with your favorite food.   T   F

CRITICAL THINKING   What problems do you think bad habits can cause? What do you think is the best way to stop a bad habit?

Pronunciation
Homophones

A 🎧2–24 **Listen and repeat.**

1. right, write   2. there, their   3. road, rode

B 🎧2–25 **Listen.** Circle the words you hear.

1. hear   here   2. know   no   3. too   two
4. I   eye   5. wear   where   6. for   four

C **Work with a partner.** Take turns to make sentences using the words in **B**.

Communication

Find out about your classmates' habits. Work in a group. Talk about the habits below. Add your own ideas. Who do you think has the best habits in your group?

DO YOU...?

eat healthy meals
clean your room
exercise
arrive on time for events
get enough sleep
go outside for fresh air
help with housework
take breaks to relax
save money

Do you eat healthy meals?

Yeah, I do.

How often do you eat healthy meals?

I try to eat something healthy twice a day.

A student climbing a wooden ladder in Hunan province, China

School children in Indonesia crossing a broken bridge

Reading

A **Look at the photos.** Where do you think these children are going?

B **Skim the first paragraph.** What do you think "commute" means?

C **Talk with a partner.** How do you go to school?

AN UNUSUAL COMMUTE

🎧 2–26

How do you travel to school? Do you usually go by bus, by car, or on foot? Around the world, some children have very unusual commutes to school.

Children from the village of Banten in Indonesia cross a river to get
5 to school every day. In the past, the children crossed a bridge over the river. But it broke after a heavy rain in 2012. For 10 months, the bridge was broken. There is another bridge they could use, but the journey is 30 minutes longer. Students usually chose to cross the broken bridge.

10 Zhang Jiawan is a village in the mountains in Hunan province, China. Children climb up and down tall wooden ladders to get to school and to go home. The ladders are not tied to the mountain, so people help to hold the ladder when someone else is climbing.

In Colombia, 11 families with school-age children live on one side of
15 the Rio Negro valley. The children's daily commute is breathtaking. 400 meters above the valley, a thick metal cable carries the children to school. A V-shaped branch slows them to about 80 kilometers an hour. It is the quickest way to get to school. But often, when it rains, the cable is too dangerous. The children stay home and can't go to
20 school.

According to UNESCO, about 57 million children around the world can't go to school. It is not easy to solve this problem, but it is something we should continue to work on.

Comprehension

A Answer the questions about *An Unusual Commute.*

1. `Main Idea` The main idea of the article is that traveling to school is _____ for some children around the world.

   a. challenging   b. expensive   c. relaxing

2. `Detail` The children in Banten used the broken bridge because the other one was _____.

   a. too old   b. too far away   c. too long

3. `Detail` Children in Zhang Jiawan _____ to get to school every day.

   a. climb rocks   b. cross a bridge   c. climb ladders

4. `Vocabulary` In line 16, a "cable" is a _____.

   a. rope   b. box   c. ladder

5. `Inference` Children crossing the Rio Negro valley use a branch to _____ of their ride.

   a. measure the distance   b. control the speed   c. change the direction

B Complete the sentences.

1. The bridge near Banten broke in 2012 because of _____.

2. Villagers in Zhang Jiawan hold the ladder when someone else is climbing because

   _____ .

3. The daily commute of children in the Rio Negro valley is breathtaking because they ride on a metal cable _____ .

4. The cable is too dangerous when it rains, so children in the Rio Negro valley

   _____ .

C **CRITICAL THINKING** **Talk with a partner.** Read the last paragraph of the article. Why do you think some children can't go to school?

Writing

Write a short paragraph.
Describe your school commute.

I usually cycle to school. I leave my house every morning at 7:30 a.m. It takes me half an hour to get to school. I cycle past shops and the park every day.

Skateistan

**ABOUT
THE VIDEO**
Some students in
Afghanistan go to a
special school.

BEFORE YOU WATCH

Look at the title and the photo. Why do you think the school is called Skateistan? Why do you think the school is special?

WHILE YOU WATCH

A **Check your answers to the Before You Watch questions.**

B **Watch the video again.** Complete the chart with information about Skateistan.

Name of school: Skateistan
Number of students:
Percentage of female students:
Examples of subjects studied:
Most popular sport:

Hanifa, a student at
Skateistan

AFTER YOU WATCH

Talk with a partner. What do you think we can learn from doing sports? What activity do you think your school should have?

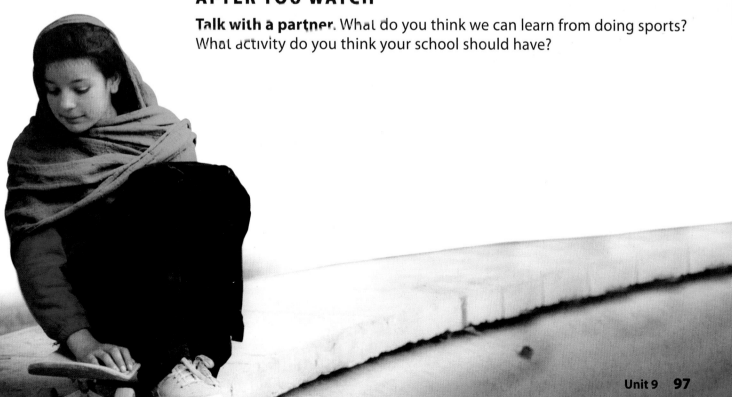

HOW DO YOU GET TO THE MALL?

Teens hanging out in the city center of Cologne, Germany

Preview

A (∩2–27) **Listen.** Label the places Akemi (**A**), Bob (**B**), Clara (**C**), and Daniel (**D**) want to go to. Two places are extra.

movie theater
____

park
____

restaurant
____

supermarket
____

museum
____

convenience store ____

B (∩2–27) **Listen again.** Circle the correct answers.

1. The movie theater is next to a (**park** / **mall**).

2. The pizza restaurant is across from the (**convenience store** / **art museum**).

3. There is a (**supermarket** / **park**) next to the museum.

4. The convenience store is behind a (**restaurant** / **movie theater**).

C **Talk with a partner.** What places in your city do you like to go to?

I always go to the café to read comics.

I go to the park every week with my friends. We like to relax and chat there.

Language Focus

A 🎧2–28 **Listen and read.** Then repeat the conversation and replace the words in blue.

REAL ENGLISH No problem.

B **Practice with a partner.** Replace any words to make your own conversation.

1. Excuse me, can you help me?
No problem. Where do you want to go?
Sure
Of course

2. I'm looking for **the art museum**.
Oh. It's on **Center Street**, across from the town square.
this restaurant / Main Avenue
the movie theater / Second Avenue

3. Uh . . . excuse me, how do you get to the **museum**?
Go straight down **Hill Street**. It's on the corner of West Avenue.
restaurant / Main Street
movie theater / King Street

4. ART MUSEUM
Hi, I'm looking for this place . . .
That's easy! **It's right behind you**!
You're right in front of it
You're right next to it

🎧2–29

GIVING DIRECTIONS		
Where's the museum?	It's	**behind** the convenience store.
		in front of the supermarket.
		next to the restaurant.
		across from the movie theater.
		between the mall **and** the park.
		on the corner of First Street.
How do I **get to** the park?		**Go straight down** Main Street.
		Go past the Internet café.
		Turn left / **right** on First Avenue.

C **Look at the map below.** Circle the correct answers.

1. The restaurant is (**on the corner of** / **next to**) Joe's Internet Café.

2. The zoo is (**across from** / **behind**) a Brazilian restaurant.

3. Kim's Korean Restaurant is (**in front of** / **between**) the 1st Avenue Theater and Center Mall.

4. Joe's Internet Café is (**on the corner of** / **between**) 3rd Avenue and Center Street.

D **2-30** **Look again at the map.** Number the directions in the correct order. Then listen and check your answers.

1. Maya is at the 1st Avenue Theater. How does she get to the zoo?

   a. _____ Go past the Brazilian restaurant.

   b. _____ Turn left on South Street.

   c. _____ Turn right on 2nd Avenue.

   d. _1_ Turn left and go straight down Center Street.

2. I'm at City Middle School. How do I get to the art museum?

   a. _____ It's on the left.

   b. _1_ Turn left and go straight down 1st Avenue.

   c. _____ Turn left on 4th Avenue.

   d. _____ Turn right on Center Street.

E **Play a guessing game.** Work with a partner. Take turns to give directions to a place in your school. Your partner guesses the place.

> Go out of the classroom and turn left. Go straight down the hall. Turn right at the computer room. Go past the art room. This place is on the left.

> Is it the boys' bathroom?

The Real World

Urban Explorer

Daniel Raven-Ellison is a National Geographic Explorer. He studies cities in a special way. He believes we can find out a lot more about the places we live in by exploring them. Instead of only learning about places through TV or books, we should also experience them ourselves.

A 🎧 2–31 **Listen.** Match Raven-Ellison's projects to their description.

1. Urban Earth ○   ○ a. drive across the United Kingdom

2. Route 125 ○   ○ b. climb tall buildings

3. Step Up Skyline ○   ○ c. walk from one side of a city to the other

B 🎧 2–31 **Listen again.** Circle the correct answers.

1. The Urban Earth project helped people to (**know / live in**) their cities better.

2. Raven-Ellison traveled across the United Kingdom to (**study different cultures / complete different adventures**).

3. He explored buildings to (**learn about the people there / do a survey**).

4. He walked the height of Mount Everest in less than (**a week / two weeks**).

CRITICAL THINKING   Do you think it's important to explore the places around us? Why or why not?

Pronunciation

O sounds

A 🎧 2-32 **Listen and repeat.**

1. movie   2. go   3. front

B 🎧 2-33 **Complete the chart.** Then listen and check your answers.

~~do~~	Tony	no	open
come	two	London	oh

Sounds like *o* in movie	Sounds like *o* in go	Sounds like *o* in front
do		

C **Work with a partner.** Take turns to read the words in **B**.

IDIOM

"A step in the right direction" is an action that brings _____ results.

a. no
b. bad
c. good

Communication

Find the places. Work with a partner. **Student A:** Look at the map below. **Student B:** Look at the map on page 133. Take turns to ask your partner for directions to each place and label them on your map. Then compare and check your maps.

mall   café
history museum   supermarket
pizza restaurant   school

How do I get to the café?

Turn left on Elm Street, then ...

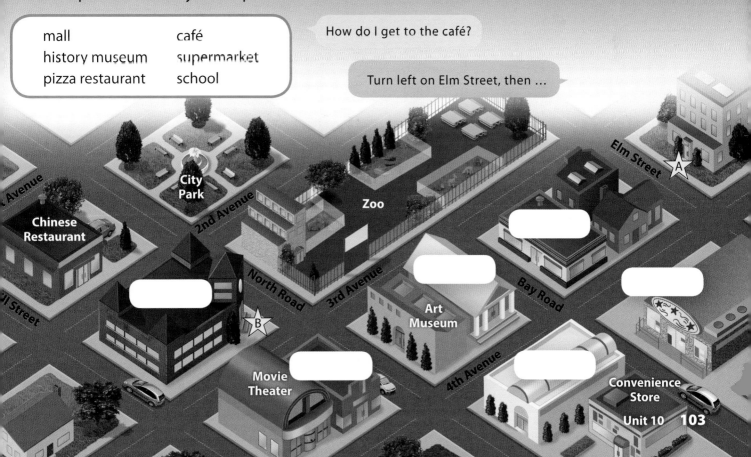

Cyclists on rented bikes in New York City

Reading

A **Skim the first two paragraphs.** Check (✓) some of the features of a bike-share system mentioned in the article.

◯ safe   ◯ use bikes for a short time
◯ convenient   ◯ easy to use

B **Scan the article.** Give an example of a bike-share system.

C **Talk with a partner.** What is the best way to explore a city?

CITIES
ON THE MOVE

🎧 2–34

Cities are usually full of people and traffic. Sometimes, traffic makes it difficult for people to get around. However, bike-share systems give people a different way to commute. In a bike-share system, people pay to use a bike for a short time. It's convenient because
5 they can get a bike from any bike station in the city. They then return it at another bike station.

These bike-share systems are very easy to use. People can use an application on their smartphones to look for bikes and to pay for them. They can also see where the bike stations are, and the number
10 of parking spaces available. Biking is a cheap and fun way of exploring the city. It's healthy and environmentally friendly, too.

Bike sharing is not new. It started in Europe in about 1965. Some of the biggest bike-share systems are the Wuhan Public Bicycle in China and Vélib' in Paris. But bike sharing is becoming more popular now. In
15 2013, there were more than 500 bike-share systems in 49 different countries. There are now almost a million bikes in bike-share systems worldwide—400,000 of them in China alone.

In the future, bike sharing may be an answer to many cities' traffic problems.

Comprehension

A **Answer the questions about *Cities on the Move*.**

1. Main Idea People _____ in a bike-share system.

   a. pay to use a bike   b. give away their bikes   c. buy their own bike to use

2. Detail Bike-share applications give users information on the _____ .

   a. weather in a city   b. location of other cyclists   c. location of bike stations

3. Inference Bike sharing is environmentally friendly because it gets people to _____ .

   a. buy bikes   b. drive less   c. share their bikes with others

4. Reference In line 11, "it" refers to _____ .

   a. biking   b. bike sharing   c. exploring the city

5. Detail Bike-share systems in _____ have the most number of bikes.

   a. France   b. China   c. the United States

B **Work with a partner.** Look at the chart below. Circle the correct answers.

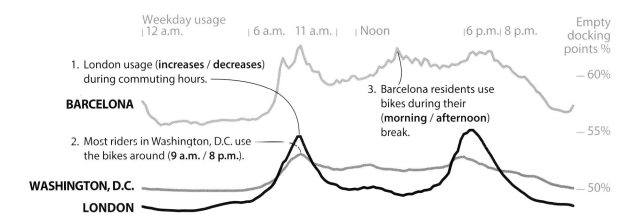

1. London usage (**increases** / **decreases**) during commuting hours.

2. Most riders in Washington, D.C. use the bikes around (**9 a.m.** / **8 p.m.**).

3. Barcelona residents use bikes during their (**morning** / **afternoon**) break.

C **CRITICAL THINKING** **Talk with a partner.** Do you have a bike-share system in your city? Do you think it is a good idea?

Writing

Write a walking tour of your neighborhood or city.

Walking Tour of London

Start your walking tour at Trafalgar Square. It's a lively place. Then visit the National Gallery on the west end of the square. This museum has a great collection of paintings. Next, go straight down . . .

VIDEO

City Walker

ABOUT THE VIDEO

National Geographic Explorer Daniel Raven-Ellison walks around cities to see how they really are.

BEFORE YOU WATCH

Complete the chart. What do you know about the cities below? Write some ideas then share them with a partner.

MUMBAI	LONDON	MEXICO CITY

WHILE YOU WATCH

A **Complete the sentences.**

For his project Urban Earth, Daniel Raven-Ellison walked across three different cities. He took a photo every (1) _____ steps. When we live in (2) _____ , there are many people and places we don't know well. Through this project, he wants people to (3) _____ their city and (4) _____ it better. He says there are (5) _____ to go on everywhere around us.

B **Watch the video again.** Check (✓) the places you hear.

◯ parks   ◯ shops

◯ streets   ◯ markets

◯ malls   ◯ restaurants

◯ museums   ◯ bridges

AFTER YOU WATCH

Talk with a partner. How well do you know your city? Which places in your city do you never visit? Why?

Daniel Raven-Ellison

Unit 10 **107**

WHAT
WERE YOU DOING?

A base jumper in
Gudvangen, Norway

Preview

A 🎧2–35 **Listen.** Circle the correct answers.

Base jumping is 1. (**an adventure sport** / **a competition**). People jump from places like 2. (**planes** / **buildings**) and mountains. They wear special suits called 3. (**skysuits** / **wingsuits**). These help them to fly in the air.

B 🎧2–36 **Listen.** Circle **T** for True or **F** for False.

1. The base jumpers jumped off a building in Norway. **T   F**

2. Rachel felt nervous when she was watching the jump. **T   F**

3. You need to have base jumping experience to do skydiving. **T   F**

4. The skills for skydiving and base jumping are similar. **T   F**

C **Talk with a partner.** Have you ever tried something risky? What did you do?

I tried ice skating for the first time.

I climbed a tree.

Language Focus

A 🎧 2–37 **Listen and read.** Then repeat the conversation and replace the words in blue.

REAL ENGLISH Hurry up!

B **Practice with a partner.** Replace any words to make your own conversation.

1

Maya, where are you? Hurry up! The movie starts in fifteen minutes!

Sorry, I **forgot to set my alarm**! I'm leaving the house now.

overslept
just woke up

2

Why didn't you set your alarm?

I was tired. I was **reading a comic** when I fell asleep.

chatting on the phone
listening to music

3

Why were you so tired?

I was **playing with** my younger cousins yesterday.

taking care of
babysitting

4

And here I am!

Um, Maya, you're still wearing pajamas!

🎧 2–38

DESCRIBING ORDER OF EVENTS	
I **was jogging when** I **fell over**.	
She **was cooking when** I **came** home.	
We **were playing** soccer **when** the rain **started**.	
Were you **eating** when she **called**?	Yes, I **was**. / No, I **wasn't**.
What **were** you **doing** last night?	I **was studying**.

C 🎧2-39 **Circle the correct answers.** Then listen and check.

1. He (**was doing** / **did**) his homework when you called.

2. They were driving home from school when they (**see** / **saw**) an accident.

3. I was out cycling when I (**was meeting** / **met**) a friend.

4. I (**was walking** / **walk**) in the park when I found a lost dog.

5. We (**were climbing** / **climbed**) a mountain when my brother hurt his knee.

IDIOM

"**It was a close shave**" **means something** _____ **nearly happened.**

a. amazing
b. interesting
c. dangerous

D **Complete the sentences.** Write your own ideas.

1. I was talking on the phone when _____.

2. I was _____ when the bell rang.

3. She was skateboarding when _____.

4. They _____ when the fire started.

5. We _____ when we heard music.

6. I was practicing the piano when _____.

E **Create a story.** Work in a group. Take turns adding a sentence. Make your story as long as possible.

I was eating dinner when I heard a knock on the door.

When I opened the door, I saw a cat.

The cat was digging a hole near a tree.

The Real World

Ice Water Diver

Rhian Waller is a National Geographic Explorer. She teaches at the Darling Marine Center in the United States. She studies animals that live in extreme places. She is very interested in corals and often has to dive in cold water to study them.

A 🎧2–40 **Listen.** Circle the correct answers.

1. Waller is a (**scientist** / **diving instructor**).

2. She studied corals on video screens because they are (**small** / **hard to reach**).

3. It's difficult to dive in Alaska because (**it's very cold** / **there are dangerous animals**).

B 🎧2–40 **Listen again.** Complete the sentences. Use the correct forms of the words in the box.

| swim | look | dark | touch | dangerous |

On one of Waller's dives, it was very (1) _____. She was (2) _____ when she got lost. She (3) _____ for the bubbles to find her way up. It was a (4) _____ experience, but she doesn't mind the risk. Now she can see the corals up close and (5) _____ them.

CRITICAL THINKING Do you think we should take risks to do something we love?

Pronunciation
Ending blends: -sk, -st, -nk, -nt

A 🎧2–41 **Listen and repeat.**

1. risk   2. think   3. lost   4. sank   5. accident

B 🎧2–42 **Listen.** Circle the sounds you hear.

1. nt   nk   4. nk   nt

2. sk   st   5. sk   st

3. st   sk   6. nt   nk

C **Work with a partner.** Take turns to read the words in the box.

| task   frank   first   apartment   desk   bank |

Communication

Play a game. Work in two groups. Pick an action from each column below. Form a sentence and take turns to read it to the other group. The other group has to act out your group's description. Add your own actions.

dance	stand up
jump	sneeze
run	laugh
sing	shout
play the guitar	fall asleep
use the computer	turn around

Sally was dancing when Alex stood up.

Grace and Tom were jumping when Mason sneezed.

Amanda Brewer was cage diving when she took this photo of a great white shark.

Reading

A **Look at the photo.** What do you think is happening?

B **Scan the article.** What did Brewer do in Mossel Bay?

C **Talk with a partner.** What do you think of sharks?

DIVING
WITH SHARKS

🎧 2–43

Amanda Brewer is an art teacher from New Jersey, in the United States. She is very interested in sharks. She even traveled to South Africa as a volunteer for White Shark Africa.

In the summer of 2014, Brewer was volunteering in Mossel Bay,
5 South Africa. She was working with scientists to collect information about sharks. She was also helping out on shark-spotting trips.

On one of these trips, Brewer dived into the ocean in a metal cage. She was hoping to see a shark up close. She didn't have to wait very long. A great white shark suddenly appeared and swam straight
10 toward the cage. It wanted to eat a piece of meat tied to the cage. Brewer managed to take a photo of the animal just when it opened its mouth.

Brewer was very excited about her experience with the shark—she said she wasn't scared at all. "They're beautiful, powerful, and
15 intelligent, and it erases all the fear," she explained. After her close encounter, she shared the photo she took online. Soon, many people were talking about it.

She also hung the photo in her classroom for her students to see. They were amazed to hear about her adventure. She hopes to use
20 the image to teach her students that we should protect sharks.

Comprehension

A **Answer the questions about *Diving with Sharks*.**

1. Main Idea The article is about ____ .

   a. a shark attack   b. dangerous sharks   c. getting close to a shark

2. Vocabulary A "volunteer" is someone who works ____ . (line 3)

   a. for many organizations   b. with animals   c. without getting money

3. Inference The shark swam to the cage because it was ____ .

   a. angry   b. hungry   c. playful

4. Detail Brewer feels ____ about her experience with the shark.

   a. scared   b. nervous   c. excited

5. Inference Brewer says we shouldn't ____ sharks because they are beautiful and intelligent animals.

   a. be afraid of   b. go near   c. feed

B **Complete the chart.** Write notes to describe Brewer's experience.

What happened?	When did it happen?	Where did it happen?	Why did she go there?
She saw a when she was			She was volunteering for

C **CRITICAL THINKING** **Talk with a partner.** Do you think we should protect sharks? Why or why not?

Writing

Write about a risk that you took. Describe what happened, what you did, and whether you think it was worth it.

Last month, I went rock climbing for the first time. I was nervous, but I decided to try it out. I had a rope, but I was scared because I was so high up. My arms and legs were shaking! I was thinking of giving up halfway. But when I finally reached the top, I was so happy. Now, I'm not so scared anymore.

Dangerous Waters

ABOUT THE VIDEO

Brady Barr is a reptile expert and TV host on the National Geographic Channel.

BEFORE YOU WATCH

What do you know about alligators? Circle **T** for True or **F** for False.

1. Alligators often attack people.　　　　　　　**T**　**F**

2. You can find alligators in the United States.　**T**　**F**

3. Another name for an alligator is "gator."　　　**T**　**F**

WHILE YOU WATCH

A **Check your answer to the Before You Watch questions.**

B **Watch the video again.** Complete the summary.

Brady Barr was walking through the (1) ＿＿＿＿＿＿＿ and water looking for an (2) ＿＿＿＿＿＿＿ . It was difficult to walk, so he decided to use a (3) ＿＿＿＿＿＿＿ . He was rowing along when suddenly he fell into the (4) ＿＿＿＿＿＿＿ !

Brady Barr and an alligator

AFTER YOU WATCH

Talk with a partner. How do you think Brady Barr felt? How would you feel? Would you like to have a job like Brady Barr?

WE'RE GOING TO
VOLUNTEER!

Preview

A **Work with a partner.** Talk about the photo using the words in the box.

clean up	trash	volunteer
beach	plastic	pick up

B 🎧 2–44 **Listen.** Check (✓) the activities that Martha and Kathy are going to do next Saturday.

- ⬜ volunteer
- ⬜ clean a beach
- ⬜ plan a charity event
- ⬜ put up decorations
- ⬜ raise money
- ⬜ guide visitors

C **Talk with a partner.** Have you ever been a volunteer? What did you do?

I collected old newspapers for recycling.

I made cards to sell at my school fair.

Teenagers taking part in Ocean Conservancy's International Coastal Cleanup

119

Language Focus

A 🎧 2-45 **Listen and read.** Then repeat the conversation and replace the words in blue.

REAL ENGLISH Definitely!

B **Practice with a partner.** Replace any words to make your own conversation.

① We're going to have the charity fair in the gym. Who's going to decorate it?

I am! I **made some awesome decorations**.

> have lots of balloons
> made some cool posters

② OK, we need music. Ming, are you going to be the DJ?

Definitely! I'm going to play some cool **hip-hop**.

> rock music
> dance music

③ Who's going to make the food?

I'm going to **bake some cookies**. Ming's going to help.

> make cupcakes
> bake a cake

④ So Stig, what are you going to do?

Well, I'm going to come to the fair and **eat the cookies**!

> dance
> have a great time

🎧 2-46

DESCRIBING FUTURE PLANS

I'm **going to volunteer** at a charity event.
She's **going to sing** at the party.
They're **going to clean up** the beach.

Are you **going to come** to the fair?	Yes, I **am**. / No, **I'm not**.
What's he **going to do**? **What** are you **going to eat**?	He's **going to play** music. I'm **going to eat** a sandwich.
When is the charity fair?	It's **tomorrow / next week**.

C Write questions for the answers.

1. What's Matt going to do _____? (**Matt / do**) He's going to make T-shirts.

2. _____? (**Ethan / volunteer**) Yeah, he is.

3. _____? (**Mary / draw**) No, she isn't.

4. _____? (**Laura / sing**) No, she's going to put up decorations.

5. _____? (**James / do**) He's going to raise money for charity.

D 🎧 2–47 **Complete the conversation.** Use the correct forms of the words in parentheses. Then listen and check your answers.

Marco: Hey Mei-Yin, are you going to the school dance?

Mei-Yin: (1) _____? (**when**)

Marco: It's on Friday, June 3rd. It starts at seven.

Mei-Yin: (2) _____ are you (3) _____ _____? (**wear**)

Marco: I don't have a suit, so I'm going to wear my brother's. What about you?

Mei-Yin: I'm (4) _____ (**wear**) the dress I bought recently.

Marco: Are you (5) _____ (**bring**) your friends to the dance? They said we could invite friends.

Mei-Yin: Yeah, I am. A few of my friends are (6) _____. (**come**)

E **Play a game.** Work in a group. Think of an activity, such as playing soccer, going to school, or sleeping. Take turns to act out preparations for the activity. Group members guess the activity that the person is going to do.

What am I going to do?

You're going to paint!

The Real World

Saving Food

Tristram Stuart is a National Geographic Explorer. He hopes to reduce the amount of food waste around the world. He's trying to get supermarkets, farms, and shops to give their unsold food to charity.

A 🎧 **2–48 Listen.** Circle the correct answers.

1. One-third of food produced (**is** / **is not**) eaten.

2. Supermarkets waste food because they only sell food that (**comes from farms** / **looks nice**).

3. Volunteers go to food businesses and farms to (**collect their extra food** / **record their food waste**).

4. Feeding the 5000 reduces food waste by giving the food to (**hungry people** / **other countries**).

B **Look at the diagram.** It shows the amount of food produced in the United States. What is wasted most? Why do you think this is?

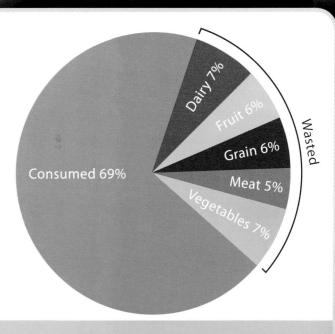

Consumed 69%

Dairy 7%
Fruit 6%
Grain 6%
Meat 5%
Vegetables 7%

Wasted

CRITICAL THINKING Does food wastage also happen at home? How does food get wasted?

Pronunciation

Reduction: *going to*

A 🎧2–49 **Listen and repeat.**

1. Lily: Are you going to raise money for the school fair?

   Carl: Yes. I'm going to sell cookies.

2. Max: Is he going to sign up for the school fair?

   Bella: No, he isn't.

B 🎧2–50 **Listen. Complete the sentences.**

1. We're _____ a school dance next week.

2. Are you _____ some money?

3. The DJ is _____ some awesome music.

4. Joe and Maria are _____ cookies and cupcakes.

5. Who's _____ posters for the dance?

C **Work with a partner.** Take turns to read the sentences in **B**.

DO YOU KNOW?

We can feed _____ people by saving one-third of the food we produce around the world.

a. 30 million
b. 300 million
c. 3 billion

Communication

Plan a school charity sale. Work in a group of three. Find out what your group members are going to do. Then complete the chart. **Student A:** Look at the chart below. **Student B:** Look at the chart on page 133. **Student C:** Look at the chart on page 134.

WHEN	STUDENT A	STUDENT B	STUDENT C
today	design a T-shirt		
tomorrow	make decorations		
next week	buy plates and cups		
on the day of the party	sell the drinks		

What are you going to do today?

I'm going to design a T-shirt.

A participant of the
Google Science Fair
showing his project

Reading

A **Look at the photo and title.** What do you think the article is about?

B **Scan the article.** Who can take part in the competition?

C **Skim the article.** What are Brittany's and Elif's projects?

INVENTING the FUTURE

🎧 2–51

Imagine you can change the world by asking yourself three questions: *What do I love? What am I good at? What do I want to change?*

The Google Science Fair is a competition for teenagers aged 13 to 18.
5 It wants them to create a project by thinking about these questions. Google hopes this competition is going to find the world's next great scientists.

Brittany Wenger, 17, found a way to improve the accuracy of a cancer-testing computer program. This program is successful about
10 97 percent of the time. Unlike other similar programs, Brittany's program is "trained." When her program does tests, it learns from experience and becomes better. Brittany plans to introduce her invention to hospitals one day. She also volunteers with a group called Made with Code. She shows other girls how they can achieve
15 their dreams through computer programming.

Turkish teenager Elif Bilgin wants to reduce pollution. So, she spent two years doing research on making plastic from other kinds of materials. She wanted to make a new kind of plastic that people can use in everyday life. Now, she found a way to make plastic using
20 banana peels! Some companies are using Elif's plastic to make artificial body parts. Elif hopes that her plastic is going to replace normal plastic in the future.

Comprehension

A Answer the questions about *Inventing the Future*.

1. `Inference` The goal of the competition is to _____ .

   a. plan science projects   b. support young scientists   c. teach teenagers science

2. `Detail` According to the article, Brittany's program is better because it _____ .

   a. is fast   b. is cheap   c. learns from experience

3. `Detail` Brittany _____ Made with Code to teach other girls how to create computer programs.

   a. set up   b. volunteers with   c. raised money for

4. `Inference` The material usually used to make plastic is _____ .

   a. too expensive   b. difficult to get   c. bad for the environment

5. `Vocabulary` The word "artificial" means _____ . (line 21)

   a. not natural   b. intelligent   c. strong

B Check (✓). Who do these sentences describe?

	Brittany	Elif
She works with computers.		
She was successful in inventing something useful.		
She wants hospitals to use her invention.		
She wants to protect the environment.		

C **CRITICAL THINKING** **Talk with a partner.** What do you want to change around you? Why?

Writing

Write a short proposal. Plan a class project or an event with a partner. Describe the project and your duties.

Project Proposal

We're going to have a sale of old items. We want to get people to recycle and reuse old materials! We're going to get everyone in our class to bring items that they have, such as clothes, books, and CDs. We're also going to make posters and flyers, and put them up around the school.

Coastal Cleanup

ABOUT THE VIDEO

Every year, many people around the world volunteer to help clean up their local beaches.

BEFORE YOU WATCH

Work with a partner. You are going to hear the numbers below in the video. Match them to what you think they describe.

1. 1,000 ○   ○ a. kilograms of trash collected worldwide

2. 500,000 ○   ○ b. kilograms of trash collected in 90 minutes

3. 3.5 million ○   ○ c. number of volunteers

WHILE YOU WATCH

A Check your answers to the Before You Watch questions.

B Watch the video again. Circle **T** for True or **F** for False.

1. The volunteers in the video help to clean up the beaches in other countries.   **T   F**

2. Some of the volunteers need to wear special clothes.   **T   F**

3. Most of the trash on the beaches comes from ships.   **T   F**

AFTER YOU WATCH

Talk to a partner. How clean are the beaches in your country? Would you volunteer to help clean them up?

A volunteer collecting trash in Paranaque, Philippines

Review Game 2

Play with 2–4 classmates. Take turns. Each classmate has a game counter. Toss a coin and move your counter.

Heads = move two squares
Tails = move one square

Can't answer? Miss a turn!

START!

1. Say three things you did last week.

2. What's wrong with this man?

3. What do you call a disease that spreads quickly to many people?

4. Using *some* and *any*, name two things that are in your refrigerator, and two that aren't.

5. When did you do something risky?

6. Give directions to the bathroom nearest to you.

7. What do you call a flat bread with cheese and tomato on it?

8. Give directions from your house to school.

9. How often do you play sports after school?

10. Give advice to a friend who has a cold.

11. What's your favorite food?

12. Your friend has a cut. What should she do?

13. What does "your eyes are bigger than your stomach" mean?

14. Unscramble this word:
n o s o p
Hint: You use it for eating.

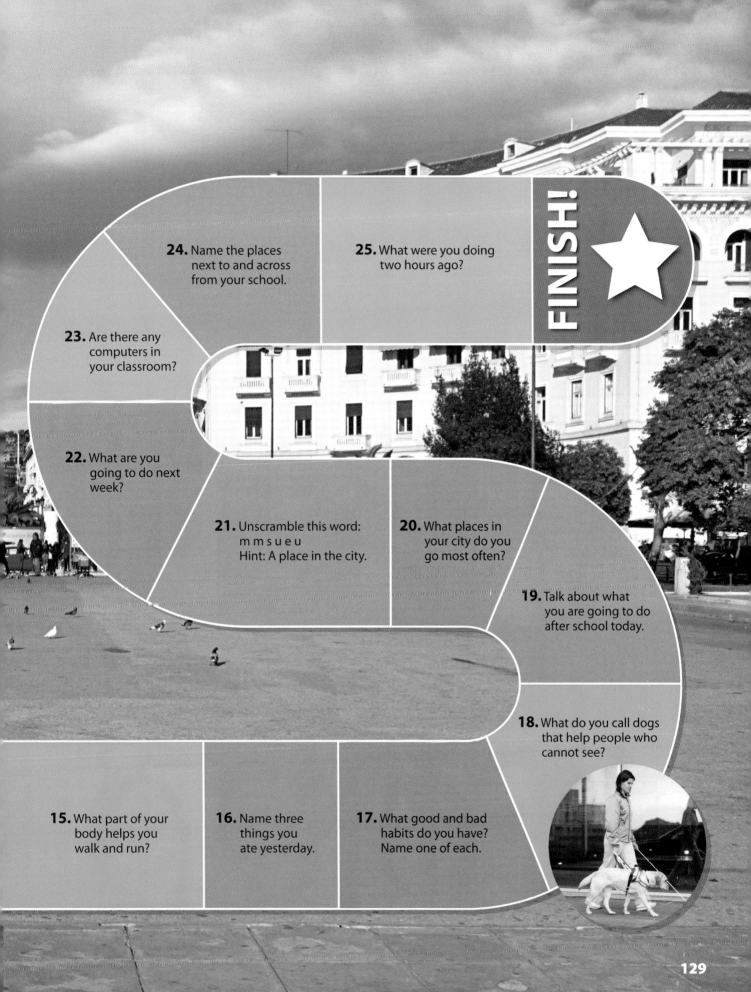

24. Name the places next to and across from your school.

25. What were you doing two hours ago?

FINISH!

23. Are there any computers in your classroom?

22. What are you going to do next week?

21. Unscramble this word: m m s u e u
Hint: A place in the city.

20. What places in your city do you go most often?

19. Talk about what you are going to do after school today.

18. What do you call dogs that help people who cannot see?

15. What part of your body helps you walk and run?

16. Name three things you ate yesterday.

17. What good and bad habits do you have? Name one of each.

UNIT 1 COMMUNICATION

Share your schedule. Complete the schedule below. Don't show your partner. Ask and answer questions about your partner's schedule.

TIME	MONDAY	TUESDAY	WEDNESDAY	THURSDAY	FRIDAY
Before school	basketball				
Morning		math			
			lunch		
Afternoon			art		science
After school				homework	

UNIT 2 COMMUNICATION

Play a guessing game. Student A: Choose one person in the photo. Don't tell your partner who it is. **Student B:** Ask yes/no questions to guess who your partner chose. Take turns.

UNIT 4 COMMUNICATION

Play a quiz game. Work with a partner. Take turns to ask and answer questions.

Student A:

QUESTIONS	ANSWERS
1. What's the highest mountain in Japan? a. Mt. Kita b. Mt. Fuji	Mt. Fuji
2. What's the hottest desert in Africa? a. the Sahara Desert b. the Taklimakan Desert	the Sahara Desert
3. What's the tallest waterfall in the world? a. Niagara Falls, U.S.A./Canada b. Angel Falls, Venezuela	Angel Falls, Venezuela
4. What's the smallest country in Asia? a. Singapore b. The Maldives	The Maldives
5. What's the windiest city in the world? a. Wellington, New Zealand b. Rio Gallegos, Argentina	Wellington, New Zealand
6. What's the coldest continent? a. Australia b. Antarctica	Antarctica
7. What animal lays the largest egg on Earth? a. Ostrich b. Emperor penguin	Ostrich
8. What country has the narrowest street in the world? a. Italy b. Germany	Germany

UNIT 6 COMMUNICATION

Take a poll. Write the names of six singers or groups. Ask your classmates to rate each one. Find out the most popular singer in your class.

SINGER OR GROUP	NAME:	NAME:	NAME:	NAME:	TOTAL POINTS

UNIT 4 COMMUNICATION

Play a quiz game. Work with a partner. Take turns to ask and answer questions.

Student B:

QUESTIONS	ANSWERS
1. What's the tallest building in the world? a. Shanghai Tower, China b. Burj Khalifa, United Arab Emirates	Burj Khalifa, United Arab Emirates
2. What's the longest river in South America? a. the Amazon River b. the Orinoco River	the Amazon River
3. What's the highest mountain in Africa? a. Mt. Kenya b. Mt. Kilimanjaro	Mt. Kilimanjaro
4. What's the largest desert in Asia? a. the Arabian Desert b. the Gobi Desert	the Gobi Desert
5. What's the biggest country in South America? a. Mexico b. Brazil	Brazil
6. Who's the tallest man in the world? a. Sultan Kösen b. Bao Xishun	Sultan Kösen
7. What's the heaviest land animal on Earth? a. African elephant b. Hippopotamus	African elephant
8. What's the saltiest ocean on Earth? a. the Indian Ocean b. the Atlantic Ocean	the Atlantic Ocean

UNIT 10 COMMUNICATION

Find the places. Look at the map below. Take turns to ask your partner for directions to each place and label them on your map. Then compare and check your maps.

Chinese restaurant   art museum

zoo   park

convenience store   movie theater

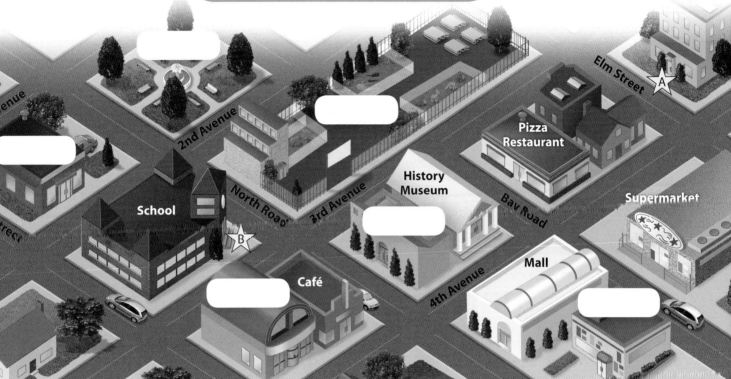

UNIT 12 COMMUNICATION

Plan a school charity sale. Find out what your group members are going to do. Then complete the chart.

Student B:

WHEN	STUDENT A	STUDENT B	STUDENT C
today		plan the entertainment	
tomorrow		buy balloons	
next week		put up decorations	
on the day of the party		make sandwiches	

UNIT 7 COMMUNICATION

Find the differences. Look at the photo below. Take turns asking and answering questions to find six differences. Circle them.

UNIT 12 COMMUNICATION

Plan a school charity sale. Find out what your group members are going to do. Then complete the chart.

Student C:

WHEN	STUDENT A	STUDENT B	STUDENT C
today			plan the poster design
tomorrow			make posters
next week			choose the music
on the day of the party			sell sandwiches

IRREGULAR PAST TENSE VERBS

BASE FORM	PAST FORM
become	became
bring	brought
buy	bought
catch	caught
choose	chose
come	came
cost	cost
cut	cut
draw	drew
drink	drank
drive	drove
eat	ate
fall	fell
feel	felt
fight	fought
find	found
fly	flew
get	got
give	gave
go	went
grow	grew
hear	heard
hurt	hurt
keep	kept
know	knew
let	let

BASE FORM	PAST FORM
lose	lost
make	made
mean	meant
meet	met
pay	paid
put	put
read	read
ride	rode
run	ran
say	said
see	saw
sell	sold
sing	sang
sleep	slept
speak	spoke
steal	stole
swim	swam
take	took
teach	taught
tell	told
think	thought
throw	threw
understand	understood
wear	wore
win	won
write	wrote

LANGUAGE NOTES

UNIT 1 WHAT DO YOU LIKE TO DO?

LIKE + INFINITIVE

| What do | you they | like to do? | I They | like to don't like to | draw. |
| What does | he she | | He She | likes to doesn't like to | play sports. |

WH- QUESTIONS (HOW OFTEN)

How often do	you they		I They	play once a week.
How often does	he she	play basketball?	He She	plays twice a week.
When do	you		I	play before school.
When does	he		He	plays after lunch.

TIME EXPRESSIONS

| once twice three times four times five times | a week a month a year | on | Mondays Wednesdays Thursdays Saturdays weekdays weekends |
| every day | | | |

UNIT 2 WHAT DOES SHE LOOK LIKE?

LOOK LIKE

What do	you they	look like?	I'm They're	tall.
			I have They have	long brown hair.
What does	he she		He's She's	medium height.
			He wears She wears	glasses.

ADJECTIVAL ORDER

Size	Style	Color	Body Part
long short	curly spiky straight	black blond brown red	hair
		blue brown green	eyes

UNIT 3 I BOUGHT NEW SHOES!

INDIRECT OBJECT PRONOUNS (WITH *GIVE, GET, BUY*)

She **gave**	me him	
He **got**	her	some clothes.
They **bought**	us them	

SUBJECT PRONOUNS / POSSESSIVE ADJECTIVES

When did	you he she we they	get	your his her our their	sneakers?	I He She We They	got them recently.

PAST TIME EXPRESSIONS

just

recently

yesterday

last night/week/month

two months/years **ago**

UNIT 4 WHAT'S THE COLDEST PLACE ON EARTH?

SUPERLATIVE ADJECTIVES

Short adjectives (1 syllable)	high low	**the** high**est** **the** low**est**
1-syllable adjectives (ending with a short vowel sound and a single consonant)	big hot	**the** big**gest** **the** hot**test**
Adjectives ending in -y	pretty windy	**the** prett**iest** **the** wind**iest**
Longer adjectives (2 or more syllables)	famous dangerous	**the most** famous **the most** dangerous
Irregular adjectives	good bad	**the best** **the worst**

UNIT 5 ARE CATS BETTER PETS THAN DOGS?

COMPARATIVE ADJECTIVES

Short adjectives (1 syllable)	clean cute	clean**er than** cut**er than**
1-syllable adjectives (ending with a short vowel sound and a single consonant)	big hot	big**ger than** hot**ter than**
Adjectives ending in -y	friendly scary	friendl**ier than** scar**ier than**
Longer adjectives (2 or more syllables)	intelligent	**more** intelligent **than** **less** intelligent **than**
Irregular adjectives	good bad	**better than** **worse than**

WH- QUESTIONS (WHICH)—COMPARATIVE ADJECTIVES

Which are **more playful**, rabbits **or** turtles?	Rabbits are **more playful than** turtles, but turtles are **friendlier than** rabbits.
	Both rabbits **and** turtles are playful.

UNIT 6 I REALLY LIKE ELECTRONIC MUSIC!

WHAT KIND OF

What kind of	music food sports movies books	do you like (the) best?	I like	rock Korean food soccer action movies science fiction	**(the) best.**

COMPARATIVES (WHICH)

Which do you like better,	hip-hop Italian food tennis	**or**	jazz? Chinese food? badminton?	I like	hip-hop Chinese food badminton	**better.**

WH- QUESTIONS (*WHO/WHAT*)

Who's your favorite singer/musician?	I like Katy Perry.
What's/**Who's** his favorite group?	He likes Green Day best.
What's their favorite kind of music?	They love rap.

UNIT 7 WHAT'S FOR DINNER?

COUNT/NON-COUNT NOUNS (*SOME/ANY*)

There	**is some** bread	in the kitchen.
	isn't any juice	
	are some cups	
	aren't any plates	

SOME/ANY QUESTIONS (SHORT ANSWERS)

Is there any fruit?	Yes, **there is.** No, **there isn't.**
Are there any bowls?	Yes, **there are.** No, **there aren't.**

NEED

What do we **need**?	We **need** some ice cream. We **don't need** any chopsticks.
	We **need** something to eat.

UNIT 8 YOU SHOULD SEE A DOCTOR!

HAVE (ILLNESSES)

I You We They	**have**	a headache. a sore throat. a fever.
He She	**has**	

HURT AND *SORE*

Verb	Adjective
My leg **hurts**. I **hurt** my leg.	I have a **sore** leg. My leg is **sore**.

SHOULD (ADVICE)

I You He She We They	**should** stay home. **shouldn't** go to school.					
Should	I he she we they	take some medicine?	Yes,	you he she we they	**should**.	
			No,			**shouldn't**.

UNIT 9 I OFTEN SKATE AFTER SCHOOL.

TENSE CONTRAST (PRESENT PROGRESSIVE AND PRESENT SIMPLE)

Are you **studying** right now?	Yeah, I always **study** for an hour after school.
What do you usually **do** after school?	I **do** my homework first, then I **play** soccer.
What are you **doing**?	I'm **watching TV**.

DESCRIBING FREQUENCY

Do you **often** go shopping?	I go shopping **once in a while**.		
	No, I	**seldom** **rarely** **hardly ever**	go shopping.

UNIT 10 HOW DO YOU GET TO THE MALL?

PREPOSITIONS OF LOCATION

Where's the museum?	It's	**across from** the park.
		behind the zoo.
		in front of the restaurant.
		next to the movie theater.
		on the corner of First Street **and** Second Avenue.
		between the park **and** the zoo.
		on the left.
		on the right.

IMPERATIVES (DIRECTIONS)

How do you **get to** the park?	**Go straight down** Main Street.
	Go past the Internet café.
	Turn left/right on First Avenue.

UNIT 11 WHAT WERE YOU DOING?

PAST PROGRESSIVE

I was He was She was You were We were They were	walking home sleeping	when the earthquake hit.
What	was he was she	doing when the storm started?
	were you were they	

UNIT 12 WE'RE GOING TO VOLUNTEER!

GOING TO FOR FUTURE

What	are you is he is she	going to do?	I'm You're He's She's We're They're	going to	make food sell books raise money	tomorrow. next month. after school.

GOING TO (SHORT ANSWERS)

Are	you they	going to put up decorations?	Yes, I am. / No, I'm not. Yes, they are. / No, they're not.
Is	he she		Yes, he is. / No, he's not. Yes, she is. / No, she's not.

FUTURE TIME EXPRESSIONS

When is it?	It's tomorrow. It's after school / soccer practice. It's this week/summer/November. It's next week/month/year. It's two days from now. It's in two months/years.

Photo Credits

1 John Coletti/JAI/Corbis, **3** EschCollection/Getty Images, **4–5** Abraham Nowitz/NGC, **6–7** Ken Redding/Ivy/Corbis, **10** Rebecca Hale/NGC, **11** BRG.photography/Shutterstock, **12–13** Kevin Scanlon/The New York Times/Redux, **13** Aaron Huey/NGC, **15** Oliver Edwards/Alloy/Corbis, **16–17** Franckreporter/iStockphoto, **19** JGI/Jamie Grill/Blend Images/Getty Images, **20** (bkg) Rebecca Drobis/NGC, **20** (cl) Cengage/NGC, **21** (tr) Jorg Hackemann/Shutterstock, **21** (b) Compassionate Eye Foundation/Martin Barraud/Taxi/Getty Images, **22–23** Cory Richards/NGC, **25** Michaela Rehle/Reuters Pictures, **26–27** Andy Richter/Aurora Photos, **29** Soren Hald/Getty Images, **30** Christ's Hospital, **32–33** Annette C. Sandberg, **33** Joey Kotfica/Moment Mobile/Getty Images, **34** Tarzhanova/Shutterstock, **35** Michael Blann/Getty Images, **36–37** Cory Richards/NGC, **37** National Geographic Maps, **39** (cl) idreamphoto/Shutterstock, **39** (c) Interpix/Alamy, **39** (c) Chris Hill/Shutterstock, **39** (cr) Bluedogroom/Shutterstock, **39** (br) Photobac/Shutterstock, **40** Nick Middleton, **41** (tr) Dea/M. Santini/De Agostini/Getty Images, **41** (b) Eric Kruszewski/NGC, **42–43** James P. Blair/NGC, **43** Robert Caputo/Aurora Photos, **44** Richard Nowitz/NGC, **45** NGC, **46–47** Hagit Berkovich/Shutterstock, **50** Dan Callister/Alamy, **51** (tr) Prochasson frederic/Shutterstock, **51** (b) Joel Sartore/NGC, **52–53** Nacho Doce/Reuters, **53** Altrendo Images/Altrendo/Getty Images, **54** Granat/Shutterstock, **55** Michael Blann/Getty Images, **56–57** Kevin Mazur/Getty Images, **59** Lonely Planet/Getty Images, **60** RGB Ventures/SuperStock/Alamy, **62–63** Camera Press/Sean Bell/ TSPL/Redux, **64** Mike Blake/Reuters, **65** (bkg) Fuse/Getty Images, **65** (t) (b) National Geographic, **66–67** (bkg) Dea/M. Santini/De Agostini/Getty Images, **66** (cl) Jacek Chabraszewski/Shutterstock, **66** (cr) Kristin Piljay/Getty Images, **67** (tr) Franckreporter/iStockphoto, **68–69** Michael Coyne/Lonely Planet Images/Getty Images, **72** Damon Winter/The New York Times/Redux, **73** (tr) KRLena/Shutterstock, **73** (b) Cengage Learning, **74–75** Red Box Pictures, **77** seagames50/Shutterstock, **78–79** Stephen Bardens/Alamy, **81** allOver images/Alamy, **82** Jonathan Torgovnik/Getty Images News/Getty Images, **83** Design Pics Inc/NGC, **84–85** Srdjan Zivulovic/Reuters, **87** Spencer Grant/Getty Images, **88–89** Jay Dickman/NGC, **90–91** (b) GILKIS - Damon Hyland/Gallo Images/Getty Images, **91** (tr) Glow Wellness/Glow/Getty Images, **92** Robert Clark/NGC, **93** Cultura RM/Fab Fernandez/Collection Mix: Subjects/Getty Images, **94–95** (bkg) Beawiharta Beawiharta/Reuters, **94** (tl) Imaginechina, **97** Skateistan, **98–99** Greg Dale/NGC, **102** Darren Moore/NGC, **104–105** John Moore/Getty Images, **107** Darren Moore/NGC, **108–109** Anders Blomqvist/Getty Images, **110–111** svetikd/Getty Images, **112** Marco Grob/NGC, **113** (tr) Mauricio Handler/NGC, **113** (b) Troy Aossey/Getty Images, **114–115** Dan Thomas/Mercury Press/Caters News, **117** Brady Barr/NGC, **118–119** Stuart Freedman/Aurora Photos, **120–121** Richard Levine/Alamy, **122** Chloe Dewe Mathews, **123** Triff/Shutterstock, **124–125** James Martin/CNET/The YGS Group, **127** Zer Cabatuan, **128–129** (bkg) photogerson/Shutterstock, (tl) Laurentiu Garofeanu/Barcroft/Getty Images, (bl) Chris McLennan Photography, **130** Franckreporter/iStockphoto, **134** Cengage Learning

NGC = National Geographic Creative

Art Credits

8, 18, 28, 38, 48, 58, 70, 80, 90, 100, 110, 120 Raketshop, **66–67, 71, 101, 103, 128–129, 133** Lachina, **Graphic Symbols: Unit 1** bioraven/Shutterstock, Abeadev/Shutterstock, **Unit 2** elenafoxly/Shutterstock, Tribalium/Shutterstock, **Unit 3** Andromina/Shutterstock, bioraven/Shutterstock, Geanine87/Shutterstock, **Unit 6** bioraven/Shutterstock, Leremy/Shutterstock, **Unit 7** Albachiaraa/Shutterstock, bioraven/Shutterstock, **Unit 10** bioraven/Shutterstock

Acknowledgments

The authors and publisher would like to thank the following individuals and organizations who offered many helpful insights, ideas, and suggestions during the development of **Time Zones**.

Asia and Europe

Phil Woodall, Aoyama Gakuin Senior High School; **Suzette Buxmann**, Aston A+; **Wayne Fong**, Aston English; Berlitz China; Berlitz Germany; Berlitz Hong Kong; Berlitz Japan; Berlitz Singapore; **Anothai Jetsadu**, Cha-am Khunying Nuangburi School; **Rui-Hua Hsu**, Chi Yong High School; **Gary Darnell**, DEU Private School, Izmir; **Hwang Soon Hee, Irean Yeon, Junhee Im, Seungeun Jung**, Eun Seok Elementary School; **Hyun Ah Park**, Gachon University; **Hsi-Tzu Hung**, Hwa Hsia Institute of Technology; **Kate Sato**, Kitopia English School; **Daniel Stewart**, Kaisei Junior and Senior High School; **Haruko Morimoto, Ken Ip**, Mejiro Kenshin Junior and Senior High School; **Sovoan Sem**, Milky Way School; **Shu-Yi Chang**, Ming Dao High School; **Ludwig Tan**, National Institute of Education; **Tao Rui, Yuan Wei Hua**, New Oriental Education & Technology Group; **Tom Fast**, Okayama Gakugeikan High School; **Yu-Ping Luo**, Oriental Institute of Technology; **Jutamas**, Prakhanong Pittayalai School; **Akira Yasuhara**, Rikkyo Ikebukuro Junior and Senior High School; **Matthew Rhoda**, Sakuragaoka Junior and Senior High School; **Michael Raship, Nicholas Canales**, Scientific Education Group Co; **Andrew O'Brien**, Second Kyoritsu Girls Junior and Senior High School; **Atsuko Okada**, Shinagawa Joshi Gakuin Junior and Senior High School; **Sheila Yu**, Shin Min High School; **Stewart Dorward**, Shumei Junior and Senior High School; **Gaenor Hardy**, Star English Centres; **Philip Chandler, Thomas Campagna**, Tama University Meguro Junior and Senior High School; **Lois Wang**, Teachall English; **Iwao Arai, James Daly, Satomi Kishi**, Tokyo City University Junior and Senior High School; **Jason May**, Tokyo Seitoku University High School; **Amnoui Jaimipak**, Triamudomsuksapattanakarn Chiangrai School; **Jonee de Leon**, Universal English Center; **Thiwaphorn Tharawatcharasart**, Uthaiwitthayakhom School; **Richard Ascough**, Wayo Women's University; **Kirvin Andrew Dyer**, Yan Ping High School

The Americas

Allynne Fraemam, Flávia Carneiro, Jonathan Reinaux, Mônica Carvalho, ABA; **Antonio Fernando Pinho**, Academia De Idiomas; **Wilmer Escobar**, Academia Militar; **Adriana Rupp, Denise Silva, Jorge Mendes**, ACBEU; **Rebecca Gonzalez**, AIF Systems English Language Institute; **Camila Vidal Suárez, Adriana Yaffe, Andrea da Silva, Bruno Oliveri, Diego A. Fábregas Acosta, Fabiana Hernandez, Florencia Barrios, Ignacio Silveira Trabal, Lucía Greco Castro, Lucy Pintos, Silvia Laborde**, Alianza Cultural Uruguay Estados Unidos; **Adriana Álvarez**, ASICANA; **Corina C. Machado Correa, Silvia Helena R. D. Corrêa, Mariana M. Paglione Vedana**, Associacao Alumni; Berlitz, Colombia; Berlitz Mexico; Berlitz Peru; Berlitz US; **Simone Ashton**, Britanic Madalena; **Keith Astle**, Britanic Piedade; **Dulce Capiberibe**, Britanic Setúbal; **Matthew Gerard O'Conner**, Britanic Setúbal; **Viviane Remígio**, Britanic Setúbal; **Adriana da Silva, Ana Raquel F. F. Campos, Ebenezer Macario, Giselle Schimaichel, Larissa Platinetti, Miriam Alves Carnieletto, Selma Oliveira**, Centro Cultural Brasil Estados Unidos CCBEU; **Amiris Helena**, CCDA; **Alexandra Nancy Lake Sawada, Ana Tereza R. P. Moreira, Denise Helena Monteiro, Larissa Ferreria, Patricia Mckay Aronis**, CELLEP; **Claudia Patricia Gutierrez, Edna Zapata, Leslie Cortés, Silvia Elena Martinez, Yesid Londoño**, Centro Colombo Americano-Medellin; **Gabriel Villamar Then**, Centro Educativo los Prados; **Monica Lugo**, Centro Escolar Versalles; **Adriane Caldas, Simone Raupp, Sylvia Formoso**, Colégio Anchieta; **José Olavo de Amorim**, Colégio Bandeirantes; **Dionisio Alfredo Meza Solar**, Colegio Cultural I; **Madson Gois Diniz**, Colegio De Aplicação; **Ilonka Diaz, Melenie Gonzalez**, Colegio Dominico Espanol; **Laura Monica Cadena, Rebeca Perez**, Colegio Franco Ingles; **Jedinson Trujillo**, Colegio Guías; **Christophe Flaz, Isauro Sanchez Gutierrez**, Colegio Iglesa Bautista Fundamenta; **Ayrton Lambert**, Colégio Il Peretz; **Samuel Jean Baptiste**, Colegio Instituto Montessori; **Beatriz Galvez, Evelyn Melendez**, Colegio Los Olivos; **Carlos Gomez, Diana Herrera Ramirez, Diana Pedraza Aguirre, Karol Bibana Hutado Morales**, Colegio Santa Luisa; **Marta Segui Rivas**, Colegio Velmont; **Thays Ladosky**, DAMAS; **Amalia Vasquez, Ana Palencia, Fernando de Leon, Isabel Cubilla, Leonel Zapata, Lorena Chavarria, Maria Adames**, English Access Microscholarship Program; **Rosângela Duarte Dos Santos**, English Space; **Walter Junior Ribeiro Silva**, Friends Language Center; **Luis Reynaldo Frias**, Harvard Institute; **Carlos Olavo Queiroz Guimarães, Elisa Borges, Patricia Martins, Lilian Bluvol Vaisman, Samara Camilo Tomé Costa**, IBEU; **Gustavo Sardo, João Carlos Queiroz Furtado, Rafael Bastos, Vanessa Rangel**, IBLE; **Graciela Martin**, ICANA (BELGRANO); **Carlos Santanna, Elizabeth Gonçalves**, ICBEU; **Inês Greve Milke, João Alfredo Bergmann**, Instituto Cultural Brasileiro Norte-Americano; **Tarsis Perez**, ICDA-Instituto Cultural Dominico Americano; **Cynthia Marquez, Guillermo Cortez, Ivan Quinteros, Luis Morales R, Melissa Lopez, Patricia Perez, Rebeca de Arrue, Rebeca Martinez de Arrue**, Instituto Guatemalteco Americano; **Renata Lucia Cardoso**, Instituto Natural de Desenvolvimento Infantil; **Graciela Nobile**, Instituto San Diego; **Walter Guevara**, Pio XII; **Juan Omar Valdez**, Professional Training Systems; **Carlos Carmona, Eugenio Altieri, Regan Albertson**, Progressive English Services; **Raul Billini**, Prolingua; **Juan Manuel Marin, Luisa Fecuanda Infort, Maria Consuelo Arauijo**, Providencia; **Carmen Gehrke**, Quatrum, Porto Alegre; **Rodrigo Rezende**, Seven; **Lcuciano Joel del Rosario**, St. José School; **Sabino Morla**, UASD; **Silvia Regina D'Andrea**, União Cultural Brasil-Estados Unidos; **Ruth Salomon-Barkemeyer**, Unilínguas Sao Leopoldo; **Anatalia Souza, Livia Rebelo**, UNIME-Ingles Para Criancas-Salvador; **Andrei dos Santos Cunha, Brigitte Mund, Gislaine Deckmann, Jeane Blume Cortezia, Rosana Gusmão**, Unisinos; **Diego Pérez**, Universidad de Ibague; **Beatriz Daldosso Felippe**, U.S. Idiomas Universe School

Jennifer Wilkin would like to acknowledge the significant contribution of the National Geographic Learning editorial team, as well as her longtime collaboration with Ian Purdon, in the writing of this series. She thanks and acknowledges her parents, who imparted a love of language through nature and nurture.